Janice VanCleave's

Oceans for Every Kid

Easy Activities that Make Learning Science Fun

John Wiley & Sons, Inc.

New York • Chichester • Brisbane • Toronto • Singapore

Illustrated by Laurel Aiello.

Library of Congress Cataloging-in-Publication Data

VanCleave, Janice Pratt.
    [Oceans for every kid]
    Janice VanCleave's oceans for every kid : easy activities that
make learning science fun / Janice VanCleave.
        p.   cm. — (Science for every kid series)
    Includes bibliographical references and index.
    Summary: Includes information on techniques and technologies of
oceanography, the topology of the ocean floor, movement of the sea,
properties of seawater, and life in the sea.
    ISBN 0-471-12454-0 (alk. paper). — ISBN 0-471-12453-2 (pbk. alk. paper)
    1. Oceanography—Experiments—Juvenile literature.
[1. Oceanography—Experiments.   2. Experiments.]   I. Title.
II. Series: VanCleave, Janice Pratt. Janice VanCleave science for
every kid series.
GC21.5.V36   1996
551.46'0078—dc20   95-9201

Printed in the United States of America

10   9   8   7   6   5   4   3   2   1

This book is dedicated to two special people in my life,
my brother and sister:
Dennis Ray Pratt and Dianne Pratt Fleming

Contents

Introduction   1

1 Drifters   5
  The Distribution of Land and Water around the Earth

2 Great Bodies of Water   13
  Identifying and Locating the Four Basic Oceans

3 Daring Travelers   23
  *The Techniques and Technology of Early Ocean
  Studies*

4 A Closer Look   31
  *The Techniques and Technology of Modern
  Ocean Studies*

5 Tools of the Trade   39
  Comparing Past and Present Oceanography Tools

6 Bumpy Bottom   49
  Learning about the Features of the Ocean Floor

7 Way Down   57
  Determining the Depth of the Ocean Floor

8 Flowing   65
  The Production and Direction of Currents

9 Up and Down   77
  Learning about Water Waves

10 Wash Out   87
    Learning How Waves Change Shorelines

11 Bulge   95
    Learning about Tides

12 Hot and Cold   103
    *Comparing the Differences in Temperature in
    Different Parts of the Ocean*

13 Squeezed   113
    Factors that Cause Water Pressure

14 Salty   121
    Why the Ocean Is Salty

15 Trashed   129
    The Problems and Solutions of Ocean Pollution

16 Dumpster   137
    *How Pollutants Affect the Life of Animals in the
    Ocean*

17 Changeable   147
    How the Oceans Affect the Earth's Weather

18 Floating Ice   157
    The Formation and Characteristics of Icebergs

19 Layered   165
    Types of Ocean Life and Their Environment

20 Sea Café   173
    *Relationships between Marine Food Producers
    and Food Consumers*

21 Bottom Dwellers 181
*Plant and Animal Life in the Different Ocean Floor
Zones*

22 Movers 189
Learning How Marine Life Moves

23 Ocean Giants 197
Learning about Whales

24 Lookers 207
Learning How Some Ocean Creatures See

25 Sensitive 217
Learning about the Sensory System of Fish

Glossary 225

More Books about Oceanography 239

Index 241

Introduction

This book is designed to teach facts, concepts, and problem-solving strategies about the world's oceans. Each chapter introduces a topic about the ocean in a way that makes learning useful and fun.

Oceanography is a branch of science that studies all aspects of the oceans' physical features and inhabitants. It is the study of anything about the oceans: the description of land surrounding them, the plants and animals that live in them, how the oceans affect humans, and how humans affect the oceans. The list can seem endless. Oceanography is not a separate science but encompasses many sciences, such as biology, chemistry, geology, physics, and geography. Few branches of scientific study depend as much on the cooperation of many researchers from different fields of science.

This book will answer questions such as "What causes high and low tides?" "What kind of life is found in the ocean depths?" "How does garbage affect sea life?" "What can you do to protect endangered marine organisms?" and "How much salt is in the ocean?"

Has all information about the oceans been uncovered and recorded? No. In fact, the oceans are the last frontier on this planet. They offer a vast wealth of material that has only begun to be tapped. With the improvement of underwater equipment and means of transportation, today's **oceanographers** (scientists who study the ocean) can study and chart ocean environments never seen before.

This book presents information about the oceans in a way that you can easily understand and use. It is designed to teach oceanography concepts so that they can be applied to many similar situations. The problems, experiments, and activities were selected for their ability to explain somewhat complex concepts. One of the main objectives of the book is to present the *fun* of learning about oceanography.

How to Use This Book

Read each of the 25 sections slowly and follow all procedures carefully. You will learn best if each section is read in order, as the information builds up as the book progresses. The format for each section is as follows:

- The chapter subtitle identifies the focus of the chapter.

- **What You Need to Know:** A definition and explanation of facts you need to understand.

- **Let's Think It Through:** Questions to be answered or situations to be solved using the information from What You Need to Know.

- **Answers:** Step-by-step instructions for answering the questions posed in Let's Think It Through.

- **Exercises:** To help you apply the facts you have learned.

- **Activity:** A project related to the facts represented.

- **Solutions to Exercises:** With a step-by-step explanation of the thought process.

In addition, this book contains:

- **Glossary:** The first time a term is introduced in the book, it will be **boldfaced** and defined in the text. The term and definition are also included in the Glossary at the end of the book. Be sure to flip back to the Glossary as often as you need to, making each term part of your personal vocabulary.

- **More Books About Oceanography:** A list of helpful books to read.

General Instructions for the Exercises

1. Read the exercise carefully. If you are not sure of the answers, reread What You Need to Know for clues.

2. Check your answers against those in the solutions and evaluate your work.

3. Do the exercise again if any of your answers are incorrect.

General Instructions for the Activities

1. Read the activity completely before starting.

2. Collect supplies. You will have less frustration and more fun if all the materials necessary for the activity are ready before you start. You lose your train of thought when you have to stop and search for supplies.

3. Do not rush through the activity. Follow each step very carefully, never skip steps, and do not add your own. Safety is of the utmost importance, and by reading each activity before starting, then following the instructions exactly, you can feel confident that no unexpected results will occur.

4. Observe. If your results are not the same as those described in the activity, carefully reread the instructions and start over from step 1.

1
Drifters

The Distribution of Land and Water around the Earth

What You Need to Know

The entire body of salt water that covers about three-fourths of the earth's surface is called the **ocean.** The distribution of ocean water throughout the earth is believed to change with time. It is generally accepted by many scientists that around 200 million years ago there was one ocean on the earth with a single land-mass in it. The landmass is known as **Pangaea** (pan-JEE-uh), which means "all land," and the ocean is known as **Panthalassa** (pan-thuh-LAH-suh), which means "all water."

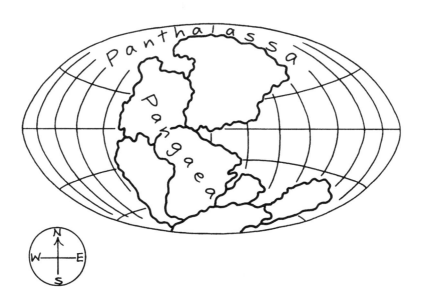

In 1911 the German scientist Alfred Wegener (1880–1930) was the first to propose the existence of Pangaea. He noticed that the **shorelines** (the area where the ocean and the land meet) of Africa and South America look like jigsaw puzzle pieces that could fit together.

No one knows exactly where Pangaea was located on the globe, but it is believed that most of the land in Pangaea was nearer to the **South Pole** (the southernmost point on the earth) than are the same landmasses today. Wegener suggested that Pangaea first split into two landmasses. He gave the northern part of Pangaea the name Laurasia, and the southern part, Gondwanaland. The body of water separating Laurasia and Gondwanaland was called the **Tethys** (TEE-thass) **Sea**. Over many millions of years, the land continued to break and drift apart, with some of the pieces drifting north and westward, and other pieces drifting north and eastward. The landmasses eventually shifted and drifted into their present-day locations.

The separation of Pangaea did not split the water forming Panthalassa into separate bodies of water, but scientists gave names to four sections of Panthalassa. The names of these four oceans are the Pacific Ocean, Atlantic Ocean, Indian Ocean, and Arctic Ocean. For information about these bodies of water, see the next chapter, "Great Bodies of Water."

Wegener was the first to propose the theory known as **continental drift.** This theory states that all the earth's landmasses were once a single body of land that separated over many millions of years and drifted apart to form what we now know as the **continents** (the seven major landmasses of the earth— North America, South America, Africa, Australia, Antarctica, Europe, and Asia). Wegener did not explain how, or why, landmasses could move, but the current explanation is that the earth's hard **crust** (thin outer layer) is split into pieces called **plates.** These plates float on a layer of softer rock beneath the crust. As plates under the ocean move apart, **magma** (liquid rock) rises, fills in the gap, and becomes solid rock as it cools.

Thus, the ocean floor widens, and landmasses that were close together move farther and farther apart. The rising and cooling of magma in the ocean floor over millions of years has formed huge underwater mountain ranges called **spreading ridges.**

While some of the crustal plates that form the ocean are spreading apart, other plates are colliding, or crashing into each other. As they collide, one plate is often pushed under the other and melts as it moves into the hotter region below. The area where plates meet, with one moving under the other, is called a **subduction zone.** Long, narrow underwater valleys called **trenches** form in these zones.

Let's Think It Through

Study the location of the animals on the diagram of Pangaea. Before Pangaea first divided, which animal, A or B, would have been in the section called Gondwanaland?

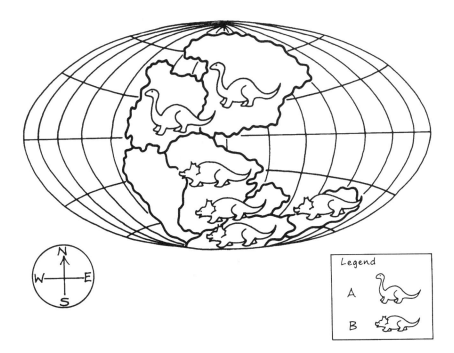

Answer

Think!

- In what part of Pangaea was Gondwanaland? The southern part.
- Which part of the diagram—upper, lower, right, or left—is south? The lower part.
- Which animal is in the southern, or lower, part of Pangaea? *Animal B would have been in Gondwanaland.*

Exercise

Study the diagram and answer the following questions:

1. Which area is Laurasia?

2. Which area is the Tethys Sea?

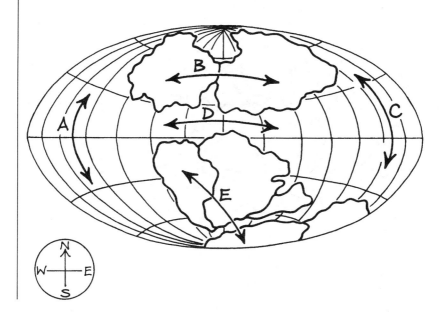

Activity: DRIFTERS

Purpose   To demonstrate how the continents drifted apart.

Materials   large shallow baking pan
tap water
9 round toothpicks
dishwashing liquid

Procedure

1. Cover the bottom of the pan with water.

2. Place 8 of the toothpicks side by side on the surface in the center of the water.

3. Wet one end of the ninth toothpick with dishwashing liquid, and put the wet end in the center of the floating toothpicks.

4. Wet the toothpick again with dishwashing liquid, and put the wet end in the center of each group of floating toothpicks.

5. Repeat step 4, wetting the toothpick before each time you put it in the center of a group.

Results When you put the toothpick with the dishwashing liquid between the 8 floating toothpicks, they separate, forming two groups with 4 toothpicks in each group. When you put the toothpick with dishwashing liquid in the center of the two groups, the toothpicks divide into four groups. Touching the toothpick with dishwashing liquid between the remaining groups results in toothpicks quickly moving away from each other.

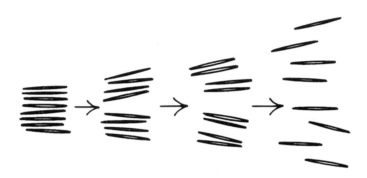

Why? The group of 8 toothpicks represents the single landmass called Pangaea, and the water in the pan represents the single ocean called Panthalassa. The first separation of the toothpicks can be compared to the breaking apart of Pangaea into a northern landmass called Laurasia and a southern landmass called Gondwanaland. While not exact, the remaining separations of the toothpicks can be compared to the formation of present-day landmasses, or continents. Laurasia is believed to have separated into the continents of North America, Europe, and Asia. Gondwanaland separated into the continents of Australia, Africa, South America, and Antarctica. The eighth toothpick represents the country of India, which broke off of Gondwanaland and, over time, moved and became attached to Asia.

Solutions to Exercises

1. *Think!*

- In what part of Pangaea was Laurasia? The northern part.

- Which part of the diagram—upper, lower, right, or left—is north? The upper part.

  Area B is Laurasia.

2. *Think!*

- Where was the Tethys Sea located? Between the northern landmass of Laurasia and the southern landmass of Gondwanaland.

  Area D is the Tethys Sea.

2
Great Bodies of Water
Identifying and Locating the Four Basic Oceans

What You Need to Know

Maps and globes show oceans as smooth blue surfaces, but beneath the surface the ocean floor is as rugged and varied as any place on the earth's land. The earth's tallest mountain, deepest canyon, and longest mountain chain are found beneath the ocean. See chapter 6, "Bumpy Bottom," for more information about the structure of the ocean floor.

Many people think of oceans as separate bodies of water. However, there are no dividing boundaries. The waters of the earth's great ocean are connected, forming a giant body of water. The areas where the land rises higher than the water are continents. Most of the land on the earth is in the **Northern Hemisphere** (the northern half of the earth), while most of the **Southern Hemisphere** (the southern half of the earth) is water.

This great ocean has four main parts, which in order of size from largest to smallest are the Pacific Ocean, Atlantic Ocean, Indian Ocean, and Arctic Ocean. (Some scientists divide the great ocean into only three parts and include the Arctic Ocean in the Atlantic Ocean.) The Arctic Ocean is so small that about 20 bodies of water the size of the Arctic Ocean would fit in the

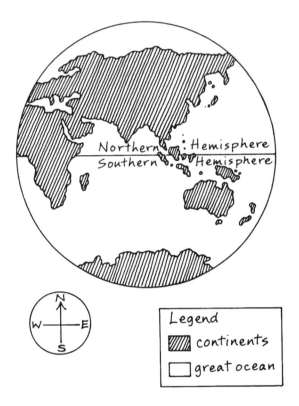

Pacific. Not only is the Arctic Ocean the smallest ocean, but much of it is covered with ice year-round.

The largest and deepest ocean is the Pacific, with a total area approximately equal to the combined areas of the three other oceans. The Pacific Ocean contains about half of the water in the earth's great ocean. Where the Pacific Ocean, Atlantic Ocean, and Indian Ocean merge is sometimes called the Antarctic Ocean or Southern Ocean.

The Atlantic Ocean is second in size to the Pacific Ocean. These two oceans are about the same length, but vary in width. At its widest point the Atlantic Ocean is about 4,375 miles (7,000 km) wide, while the Pacific Ocean is about 12,500 miles (20,000 km) wide.

The Indian Ocean is only slightly smaller than the Atlantic, but the Indian Ocean is much deeper than the Atlantic.

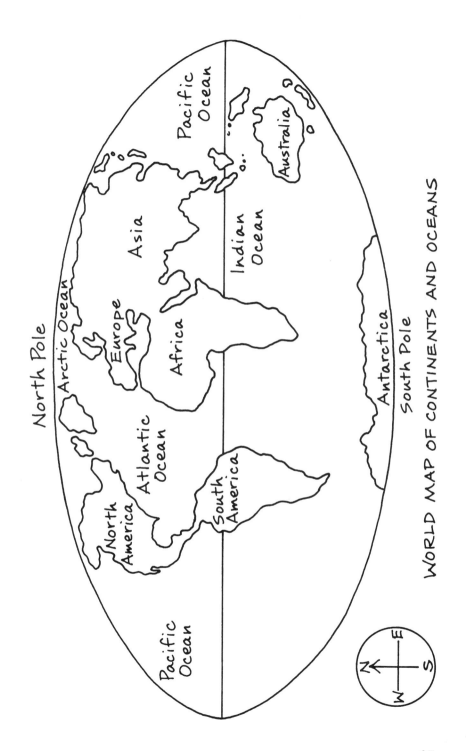

WORLD MAP OF CONTINENTS AND OCEANS

North Pole

Pacific Ocean

Arctic Ocean

Asia

Europe

Africa

Atlantic Ocean

North America

South America

Pacific Ocean

Indian Ocean

Australia

Antarctica

South Pole

N
E
W
S

15

The words *sea* and *ocean* are often used to mean the same thing, but they actually differ in meaning. The word *ocean* is included in the names of the four oceans—the Atlantic Ocean, Arctic Ocean, Indian Ocean, and Pacific Ocean. **Seas** are large bodies of salt water, but they are smaller than oceans and may or may not be part of an ocean.

Let's Think It Through

1. A **strait** is a narrow body of water that joins two larger bodies of water, such as two oceans, two seas, or an ocean and a sea. A **bay** is part of a larger body of water that cuts into a shoreline, forming a curve. Use the map to identify the following:

   a. Strait of Gibraltar

   b. Bay of Biscay

Answers

1a. *Think!*

- Which location, A or B, is a narrow channel of water connecting an ocean with a sea?

  B is the Strait of Gibraltar.

b. *Think!*

- Which location, A or B, is part of an ocean that cuts into the shoreline, forming a curve?

  A is the Bay of Biscay.

Exercises

1. Use the map to answer the following questions:

  a. How many straits connect the Sea of Japan with other bodies of water? (*Hint:* There is more than one.)

  b. The Korea Strait is between Korea and Japan. With what body of water does it connect the Sea of Japan?

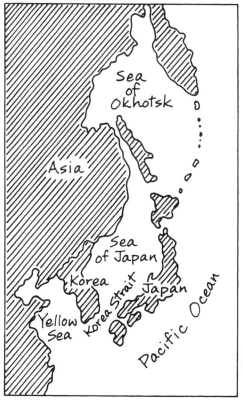

2. Seas are large bodies of salt water, but they are smaller than oceans and may or may not be part of an ocean. Use the map to name a sea that is part of the Atlantic Ocean.

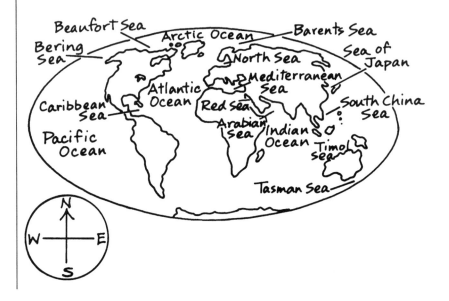

Activity: DIFFERENT AREAS

Purpose To show how two oceans can contain almost the same amount of water even though one has a larger surface area.

Materials two 12-by-12-inch (30-by-30-cm) pieces of
        aluminum foil
        ruler
        2 cups (500 ml) tap water
        helper

Procedure

1. Make a shallow box out of one of the pieces of foil following these steps:

- Fold the foil in half twice to make a 6-by-6-inch (15-by-15-cm) square.

- Fold up about ¾ inch (1.9 cm) on each edge of the foil square to make the sides of the box.

- Fold each corner of the foil to one side so that it is snug against the sides of the box.

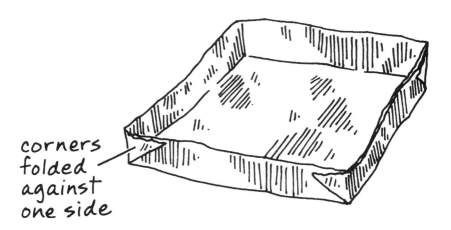

corners
folded
against
one side

2. Make a cone out of the second piece of foil following these steps:

- Fold the foil in half twice to make a 6-by-6-inch (15-by-15-cm) square.

- Bring two adjacent (neighboring) sides of the square together.

- Fold about ¼ inch (0.63 cm) of the two sides down, pressing the fold flat.

- Fold and press the foil flat again.

- Use your fingers to shape the foil into a cone.

- Fold the tip of the cone up, pressing the fold flat to seal the bottom.

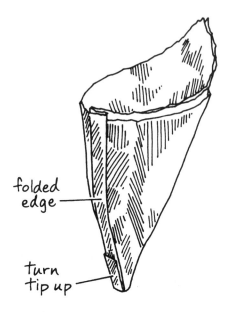

folded
edge ——

turn
tip up —

3. Compare the **area** (the size of a surface) of the open end of
   the cone with the area of the open end of the box by standing the cone, open end down, in the box. Then remove it.

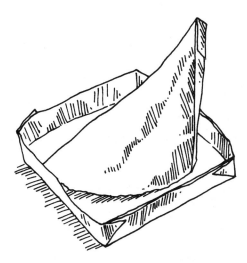

4. Set the box in a sink, and pour enough water into the box to
   fill it.

5. Ask your helper to hold the cone upright over a sink.

6. Being careful not to spill the water, pour as much of the water from the box into the cone as will fit.

7. Make note of the amount of water left in the box, if any.

Results   The open end of the box is large enough to hold the open end of the cone with room to spare, but almost all of the water from the box can be poured into the cone.

Why?   The cone and box have different open-end areas, but their **volume** (the amount of space inside an object) is almost the same. Even though the open end of the cone is smaller than that of the box, its depth is much greater. Thus, the cone can hold about the same amount of water as can the box. Like the box and cone, the Atlantic Ocean has a larger surface than does the Indian Ocean, but they contain nearly the same amount of water. This is true because the Indian Ocean, which has an average depth of 13,000 feet (3,900 m), is deeper than the Atlantic Ocean, which has an average depth of 11,000 feet (3,300 m).

Solutions to Exercises

1a.   *Think!*

- How many narrow channels of water connect the Sea of Japan with other bodies of water?

  There are five straits connecting the Sea of Japan with other bodies of water.

b.   *Think!*

- What body of water is at the other end of the Korea Strait from the Sea of Japan?

The Korea Strait connects the Sea of Japan with the Yellow Sea.

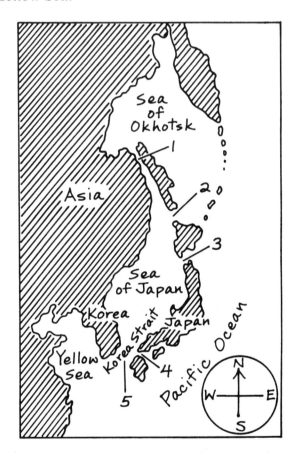

2. *Think!*

- Which sea has water from the Atlantic Ocean flowing into it?

The Caribbean Sea, Mediterranean Sea, or North Sea are parts of the Atlantic Ocean.

3
Daring Travelers
The Techniques and Technology of Early Ocean Studies

What You Need to Know

Up until the late 1400s, people were curious about what was beyond the ocean, but few were brave enough to venture out into what was at the time called the "Sea of Darkness." While sailing ships were used on rivers and along the coastlines of Mesopotamia, now known as Iraq, as early as 5000 B.C., only the most daring explorers traveled ocean waters far from shore. This is not too hard to understand since people at this time thought that the world was flat and ships would fall off the edge. Plus, giant monsters were believed to pull ships into the depths and eat the people on board.

The idea that the earth is a **sphere** (shaped like a ball) and not a cookie-shaped disk was proposed about 530 B.C., but it was more than a thousand years before this idea was generally accepted. Even so, there were those who, out of curiosity or the need or desire to find food, wealth, or power, set sail for the unknown. Regardless of the reason, these people were brave to travel without charts, weather maps, or any knowledge about the new areas they were sailing into. Many of the early voyages resulted in the discovery of new lands and more knowledge about the ocean.

Without compasses or other modern instruments, early **navigators** (directors of ships) used signs from nature to determine the position of their ships. Some used the color of the water, the smell of the air, or the presence of birds or clouds to detect land. They also used the sun and the stars to determine their general direction of travel.

During the day, navigators observed the apparent path of the sun across the sky from sunrise to sunset. Since the sun appears to rise and set in about the same direction each morning and night, it was used to judge direction. At night, stars were used to determine direction. At different locations, the **constellations** (specific arrangements of a group of stars) were seen differently. These early travelers were not familiar with terms such as **latitude** (imaginary lines encircling the earth in an east-west direction), **equator** (latitude line around the center of the earth), and **North and South Poles** (areas of the earth that are farthest north and south, respectively, of the equator). However, they noticed that when they sailed in the same latitude, judged by sailing toward the rising or setting sun, most of the same stars were seen each night. The constellations changed if they sailed at an angle to the rising or setting sun because they were changing latitude. This is because the earth is a sphere, so stars are blocked from view when they set below the **horizon** (the imaginary line where the sky meets the earth).

In the Northern Hemisphere, **Polaris** (the North Star, directly above the North Pole) can also be used to determine latitude. At the North Pole, this star appears to be directly overhead, but as one progresses toward the equator, the star appears lower in the sky. The closer Polaris is to the horizon, the smaller the degree of latitude and the closer one is to the equator. In the Southern Hemisphere, south of the equator, the constellation called Crux, or Southern Cross, is used as a rough navigational aid because the long arm of the cross points toward the South Pole.

Around 1415, western Europeans, beginning with the Portuguese, began to venture into the Atlantic Ocean. The Portu-

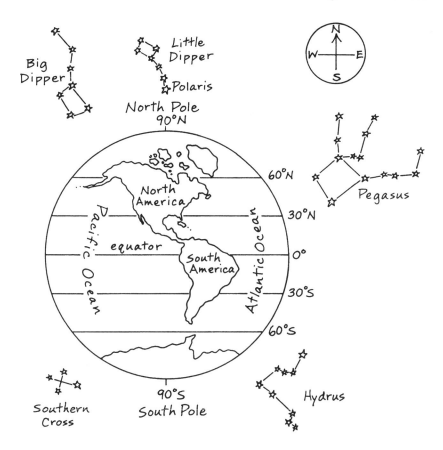

guese are credited with a technique for determining latitude by measuring the **altitude** (the angle between a heavenly body, such as a star or planet, and the horizon) of Polaris. It was determined that the altitude of Polaris is equal to the latitude of the observer. The latitude at the equator is zero degrees (0°), and the latitude at the North Pole is 90 degrees (90°). The North Pole is at 90 degrees north latitude (90° N). The higher the North Star appears in the sky, the greater the degree of latitude, and thus the closer one is to the North Pole.

The Portuguese navigators discovered that the North Star is not visible south of the equator. They solved this problem by using the altitude of the sun at noon to determine latitude. Because the sun appears to be directly overhead at noon at the equator, the altitude of the sun is greatest at the equator and decreases as one nears the South Pole.

Let's Think It Through

The diagrams represent the positions of two ships at noon. Which ship is closer to the equator?

Answer

Think!

• The sun appears to be directly overhead at noon at the equator.

• Which diagram shows the sun closer to being overhead?

Ship A is closer to the equator.

Exercise

The stars in the diagram show the position of Polaris at three different latitudes. Which position indicates that the ship is closest to the North Pole?

Activity: WHERE ARE YOU?

Purpose To use the position of the North Star to determine your latitude.

Materials 12-inch (30-cm) piece of string
protractor
metal washer
masking tape
marking pen
drinking straw
flashlight
helper

Procedure

1. Tie one end of the string through the hole in the center of the protractor.

2. Attach the free end of the string to the washer.

3. Tape the straw along the straight edge of the protractor.

4. Without covering the lines, place pieces of tape on the protractor and write 0 to 90 on the pieces as shown.

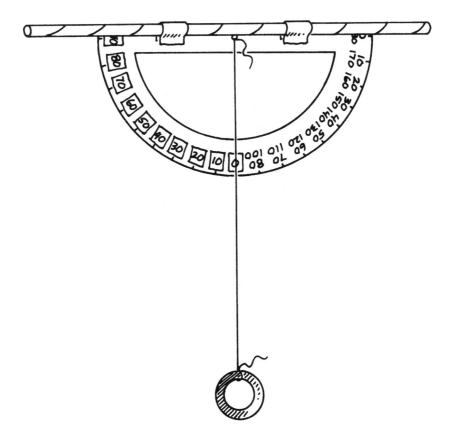

5. Stand outside and find the North Star (Polaris) by lining up the two outermost stars in the bowl of the Big Dipper. The North Star is directly ahead.

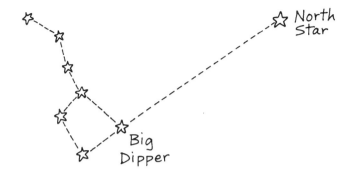

6. Close one eye and use the other to look through the straw at the North Star.

7. Ask your helper to use the flashlight to read the angle where the string crosses the protractor.

Results   The angle of the North Star above the horizon varies depending on where you are in the Northern Hemisphere. The angle will be greater the farther north you are.

Why?   The angle of the North Star above the horizon is the same as the latitude of the observer. For the child in the diagram, the **astrolabe** (instrument used to determine latitude), constructed in this experiment, shows the North Star to be about 60° above the horizon, which is where the North Star appears to this observer standing 60°N. Should the observer move to 40°N, the North Star could be seen in the northern sky 40° above the horizon. Early navigators used the altitude of Polaris to determine their location.

Solution to Exercise

Think!

- The higher Polaris is in the sky, the closer the observer is to the North Pole.

- In which position is Polaris highest in the sky?

  The ship is closest to the North Pole when Polaris is observed to be in position A.

4

A Closer Look

The Techniques and Technology of Modern Ocean Studies

What You Need to Know

The first ocean explorers were sailors who collected information that affected their voyages, such as winds, currents, and water temperature. It wasn't until the mid-nineteenth century that scientists began to study the ocean deliberately. From 1842 until 1861, Matthew Maury (1806–1873) of the United States Navy collected and published information about the entire ocean, such as data about the ocean depths, bottom material, and living things. An important result of Maury's studies was information about the general location and direction of surface currents in the ocean. Maury is often called the founder of oceanography.

From 1872 to 1876, a team of scientists under the leadership of Sir Charles Wyville Thomson (1830–1882) on board the British ship H.M.S. *Challenger* not only studied winds, currents, and temperature, but made the first scientific exploration of the ocean bottom. Buckets suspended from ropes were dropped to see what could be dragged up from the ocean floor. Deep-sea fish never seen before were caught during this expedition. In 1895, Sir John Murray (1841–1914) published a report of the expedition, in which he described the ocean bottom and provided huge amounts of information about **marine** (having to do with the ocean) life and bottom **sediments** (materials that settle to the bottom of a liquid).

The word *oceanography* was used for the first time in Murray's 50-volume report about the *Challenger* studies. This report was the starting point for the study of oceanography, which includes **marine biology** (the study of ocean life), **chemical oceanography** (the study of ocean water and its chemical characteristics), **physical oceanography** (the study of water movement in the ocean), and **geological oceanography** (the study of the ocean floor, beaches, and ocean fossils).

Modern oceanographers (scientists who study the ocean) would find the equipment used on the *Challenger* very primitive, but some of the techniques are still used, such as collecting biological samples in nets and bringing up material from the ocean bed.

Today, besides surface vessels, **submersibles** (vessels capable of going under water) and diving suits are designed to study the ocean. Submersibles have strong outer hulls to withstand the pressure of water, which increases with depth. Some of the craft have mechanical arms, viewing ports, external lights, cameras, and other instruments to help scientists observe and collect samples. While many submersible vessels have scientists inside, some do not and instead are operated from a surface ship. These underwater robots are called **ROVs** (*r*emotely *o*perated *v*ehicles).

The French marine explorer Jacques Cousteau (1910-) and Emile Gagnan, an engineer, invented a kind of diving gear that completely changed underwater diving. They invented **scuba** gear (*s*elf-*c*ontained *u*nderwater *b*reathing *a*pparatus). This gear contained compressed air in a tank worn on the back of the diver. Having an air supply, the diver could dive deeper and stay under water longer.

While much of the ocean floor is still unexplored, much more information has been collected in recent years because of new technology and methods of studying the ocean. **Bathyscaphes** are diving machines that allow scientists to reach deep parts of the ocean. Modern diving suits allow divers to work for longer periods under water. These suits can be heated, and they use battery-operated motors to get around more quickly.

Let's Think It Through

Study the diagram and determine which figure represents an ROV.

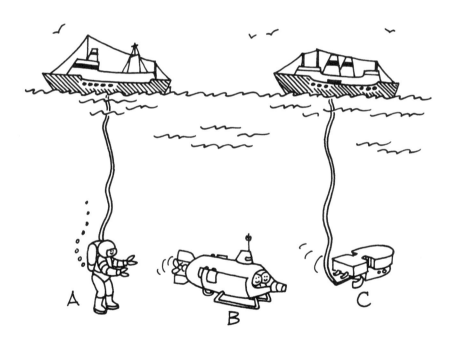

Answer

Think!

• ROVs are unmanned submersibles.

- Which diagram indicates a submersible without a person inside?

Figure C is an ROV.

Exercises

1. Study the map showing the voyage of the H.M.S. *Challenger* to answer the following questions:

   a. Where did the *Challenger's* voyage begin?

   b. What oceans were studied? List these oceans in the order in which they were studied.

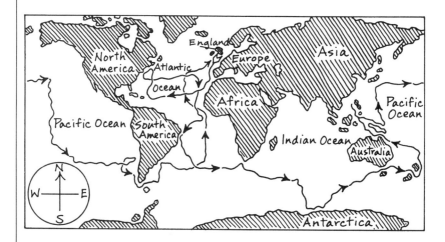

2. The deepest point on the earth lies in the Pacific Ocean in an area called Challenger Deep. Use the chart on the next page to determine the name of the three-man bathyscaphe that in 1960 reached the bottom of Challenger Deep, at about 36,000 feet (10,800 m).

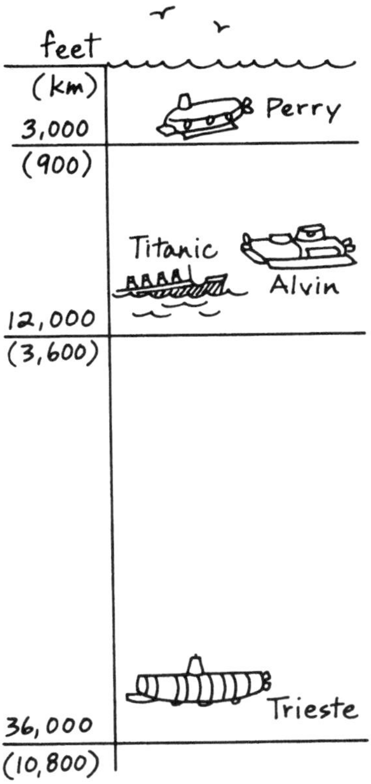

feet
(km)
3,000
(900)

Perry

12,000
(3,600)

Titanic
Alvin

36,000
(10,800)

Trieste

Activity: COMING UP!

Purpose   To demonstrate how a submarine can be made to rise.

Materials   tape
2 pennies
small narrow-mouthed plastic bottle
scissors
flexible drinking straw
modeling clay
large bowl
tap water
adult helper

Procedure

1. Tape the pennies side by side to the outside bottom of the bottle.

2. Ask an adult to use the point of scissors to make a row of three holes down one side of the bottle.

3. Place the short end of the straw into the mouth of the bottle and secure with clay.

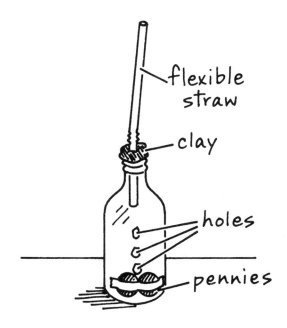

4. Fill the bowl with water.

5. Place the bottle in the bowl, holes down.

6. Hold the bottle beneath the water until it fills with water and remains on the bottom of the bowl.

   NOTE: If the bottle does not sink, add more coins.

7. Blow into the straw.

Results The bottle rises to the surface.

Why? A **submarine** is a submersible designed to operate under water for long periods of time. In 1620, the first submarine, built by Cornelius Drebell (1572–1634), a Dutchman, was sailed along the river Thames through London. This submersible was a rowboat covered with leather to keep the water out. The first submarine similar in shape to modern submarines was built in 1800 by Robert Fulton (1765–1815), an American inventor. Fulton's submarine, as well as modern submarines, surfaced and sank due to the amount of seawater in **ballast tanks** (heavy tanks used to stabilize and control the depth of submersibles). When the tanks are filled with seawater, the craft sinks, as did the bottle in this experiment. And, like the bottle, when air is used to force water out of the tanks, the submarine floats to the surface.

Solutions to Exercises

1a. *Think!*

- A winding arrow is used to show the *Challenger's* route, with the tail of the arrow at the starting point of the route and the head at the end.
- Where is the tail of the arrow?

  The Challenger's *route began in England.*

b. *Think!*

- Starting at England, follow the arrow and record the oceans in the order in which they were entered.

  The oceans, in the order in which they were studied during the Challenger's *voyage, are: Atlantic Ocean, Indian Ocean, and Pacific Ocean.*

2. *Think!*

- Find 36,000 feet (10.800 m) on the chart.
- What is the name of the vessel at this depth?

  The bathyscaphe Trieste *reached the bottom of Challenger Deep.*

5
Tools of the Trade

Comparing Past and Present Oceanography Tools

What You Need to Know

The first scientific attempt to measure the depth of the ocean was during the voyage made by the *Challenger* expedition between 1872 and 1876. (See chapter 4, "A Closer Look" for more information about this voyage.) The method was to weight one end of a rope or cable and then lower roll after roll of the rope or cable into the water until the weight hits bottom. The length of material lowered into the water was recorded and then raised and rewound in order to repeat the process in another location. Few readings were made because the tools used were not accurate and the measurements required long hours of work. Often, the weight of the rope or cable and the pressure of the water broke the line.

A similar early method of measuring depth was called **sounding.** Knots were tied in a rope at intervals of 1 **fathom** (6 feet, or 1.8 m). A weight was tied at one end of the rope and dropped over the side of the ship. The number of knots that went over the side before the weight struck bottom was counted. The number of knots equaled the depth in fathoms.

A modern method of measuring ocean depth is with **sonar,** a system that sends **ultrasound** (high-frequency sounds that hu-

mans cannot hear) from a ship's bottom to the ocean floor.
Sound is a form of energy that causes a disturbance in materials, such as water, as it travels through it. This disturbance is
called a **sound wave.** Ultrasound from the sonar device travels
through the water and is reflected back from the ocean bottom
to the ship, where a computer uses the **echo time** (the time it
takes sound waves to travel to an object, be reflected, and return) to determine the depth from the ship to the ocean bottom.

For more information about measuring ocean depth, see chapter 7, "Way Down."

Early ocean explorers relied on luck when collecting many of their samples. Nets, buckets, and hooks were dragged through the water and across the ocean bottom in an effort to bring up deep-sea organisms and objects. While nets are still used to catch fish, a special collecting net made of extremely fine mesh is now used to capture **microscopic organisms** (living beings that are too small to be seen with the naked eye). Buckets and hooks have been replaced with corers and Nansen or Nisken bottles. A **corer** is an instrument used to cut a tubular sample from the earth's crust. It consists of a hollow tube that is lowered to the ocean floor by a steel cable and driven in by a heavy weight. The corer and sample, which may include organisms from the ocean floor, are then returned to the ship and the contents of the tube studied. The **Nansen** (or **Nisken**) **bottle** is a tubelike device that can be opened and closed at different depths from the ship. Samples of water can be collected at specific levels below the ocean's surface, returned to the ship, and their temperature and other characteristics studied.

The speed of **ocean currents** (large streams of ocean water that move continuously in the same direction) was determined in the past by throwing a floatable object into the water. A rope was tied to one end of the object. The speed of the current could be determined by seeing how much rope was let out in a given time. One modern tool for determining current speed is called a **current meter.** This instrument has a propeller that is turned by the moving water. The number of turns made by the propeller per unit of time is recorded by the instrument and the speed of the current determined.

Let's Think It Through

1. For each of the two tools shown, choose one description that describes its use.

   a. determines the location of the fastest ocean currents

   b. collects sediment from the ocean floor

   c. gathers microscopic organisms

   d. measures ocean depth

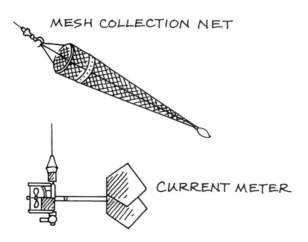

MESH COLLECTION NET

CURRENT METER

Answers

1. *Think!*

- A mesh collection net has extremely small holes to hold in microscopic materials.

The mesh collection net gathers microscopic organisms.

Think!

- A current meter is used to measure the speed of ocean currents.
- The meter can be used to measure the currents throughout the ocean.

The current meter determines the location of the fastest ocean currents.

Exercise

1. Identify and name each tool needed to perform the following tasks:

   a. compares living organisms with organisms that have died and fallen to the ocean floor

   b. determines the temperature of water at 200 feet (60 m)

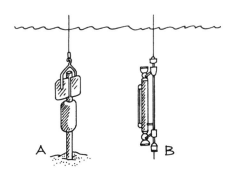

Activity: SPEEDY

Purpose   To demonstrate the method used by early sailors to determine the speed of ships.

Materials scissors
yardstick (meterstick)
11-foot (3.3-m) cord
pencil
stopwatch
helper

Procedure

1. Cut 9 feet (2.7 m) of cord, and tie a knot in each end.

2. Cut eight 3-inch (7.5-cm) pieces of cord.

3. Tie one short piece of cord at each 12-inch (30-cm) interval along the long piece of cord.

    NOTE: Tie the short pieces tight enough so that they do not slide along the string.

4. Wind the long piece of cord around the center of the pencil.

5. Hold the pencil in both hands and the wound cord loosely between the thumb and index finger of one hand.

6. Ask your helper to hold the free end of the cord and start the stopwatch.

7. When your helper says, "Go," slowly walk away backward from your helper, allowing the cord to unwind and counting the knots on the cord as they pass between your thumb and index finger.

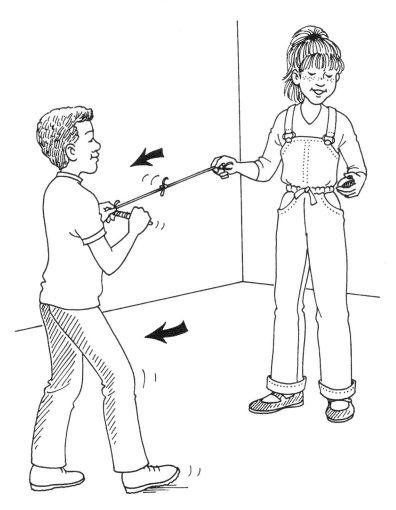

8. Stop when your helper informs you that 2 seconds have passed.

9. Rewind the cord onto the pencil and repeat steps 5 through 8, but this time walk as fast as you can.

10. Compare the amount of cord unwound each time.

Results The number of knots passing through your fingers is fewer when you walk slow than when you walk fast.

Why? In this experiment, counting the knots as you moved at different speeds is similar to the method that sailors in the past used to determine the speed of their ship. Knots were tied at regular intervals along the rope, and a log was tied to one end of the rope. When the rope was thrown overboard, the floating log and rope trailed behind the moving ship. A sailor counted the number of knots that passed through his hands in a given time. As with the number of knots that passed through your hands as you walked faster, the more knots that passed through the sailor's hands, the greater the speed of the ship. Sailors used the word *knot* to measure the speed of the ship. The word is still used today. A **knot** is 1 nautical or sea mile per hour. A **nautical mile** equals 6,076 feet (1,823 m).

Solution to Exercise

1a. *Think!*

- Instrument A has been driven into the ocean floor to collect a sample.

- Living organisms and those that have died and fallen to the ocean floor are in the sample.

Instrument A is a corer.

b. *Think!*

- Instrument B has been lowered into the water to collect a sample.
- What instrument can collect water at different depths so that its temperature can be measured?

Instrument B is a Nansen bottle.

6
Bumpy Bottom

Learning about the Features of the Ocean Floor

What You Need to Know

The ocean bottom, like the surface of the continents, is not entirely smooth, but has many irregular or bumpy features. A side view of the ocean floor might look somewhat like the diagram shown. Starting at the shoreline is the **continental shelf.** This part of the ocean floor is actually an underwater extension of the continent. The surface of the continental shelf usually slopes gently downward. The boundary of this shelf is determined by water depth. The outer limits of the shelf extend to a depth of about 667 feet (200 m). The width of the shelf varies. The continental shelf along the Pacific coastline of the United States is very narrow, with some regions having no continental shelf. However, off the coast of Boston, the shelf is about 260 miles (416 km) wide.

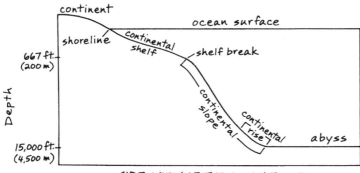

SIDE VIEW OF THE OCEAN FLOOR

The point where the continental shelf ends and the **continental slope** (the steep slanted area between a continental shelf and the deepest part of the ocean floor) begins is called the **shelf break**. At this point, the slope suddenly begins to get steeper until it reaches the great depths of the ocean floor, called the **abyss**, which has an average depth of approximately 15,000 feet (4,500 m). The bottom area of the continental slope that gently rises above the abyss is called the **continental rise**.

Part of the abyss is made of a flat surface called **abyssal plains**, while other parts contain single underwater mountains called **seamounts.** A seamount with a flat top is called a **guyot.** A series of seamounts and V-shaped, narrow, deep valleys, called trenches, form a long underwater **mountain range** (a string of connected mountains), or **ridge.** A central valley running the length of a ridge is called a **rift valley**.

The longest continuous mountain range on earth is beneath the ocean. Mountain ranges from each of the four oceans connect, forming a gigantic mountain system called the **oceanic ridge**.

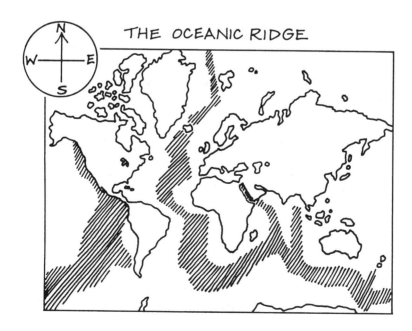

THE OCEANIC RIDGE

This long continuous mountain range has a length of about 40,600 miles (65,000 km), which is approximately one and a half times the earth's **circumference** (the distance around). The ridge rises to about 1¼ miles (2 km) above the ocean floor in most areas, but some of the seamounts are about 4 miles (6.4 km) high, and in places extend above the surface of the water. This type of seamount is called an **island** (a piece of land smaller than a continent and surrounded by water). The width of the oceanic ridge varies from approximately 300 to 1,200 miles (480 to 1,920 km).

The section of the oceanic ridge in the Atlantic Ocean, called the **Mid-Atlantic Ridge**, is the best known and the most carefully studied. The rift valley of the Mid-Atlantic Ridge appears to be an area of weakness in the earth's crust and is an area of earthquake activity. Scientists have discovered, by studying the rocks on either side of this rift valley, that the Mid-Atlantic Ridge is growing larger by about 1 inch (2.5 cm) per year.

Let's Think It Through

Study the diagram and determine which area is the continental rise.

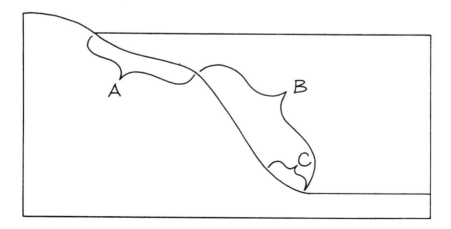

Answer

Think!

- The area in bracket A is an underwater extension of the continent. This is the continental shelf.

- The area in bracket B is a steep slope connecting the continental shelf with abyss. This is the continental slope.

- What part of the continental slope gently rises from the abyss?

  Area C is the continental rise.

Exercises

1. Identify the ocean floor features in the diagram.

2. Match the seamounts in the diagram on the next page with the following descriptions of underwater features and name them:

a. a seamount with a flat top

b. a seamount extending above the ocean's surface

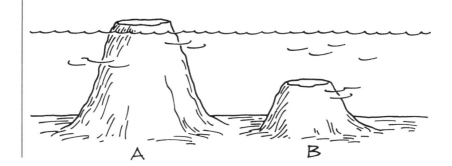

Activity: DOWN UNDER

Purpose   To make a model of the features of the ocean floor.

Materials   scissors
medium-size cardboard box
ruler
aluminum foil
2 cups (500 ml) tap water
blender
newspaper page
large tea strainer
sponge
¼ cup (63 ml) flour
adult helper

Procedure

1. Ask an adult to cut the box down to a height of about 2 inches (5 cm).

2. Line the bottom and sides of the box with aluminum foil.

3. Pour the water into the blender.

4. Tear the newspaper page into small pieces.

5. Add the newspaper pieces to the blender, and put the lid on the blender.

6. Ask an adult to turn on the blender and blend the water and paper until a gray pulp is produced.

7. Hold the strainer over the sink, and ask an adult to pour the pulp into the strainer.

8. Press the pulp into the strainer with your fingers to remove as much water as possible.

9. Place the pulp in the foil-lined box and begin shaping it into the features of the ocean bottom.

10. If you need more pulp, repeat steps 3 through 9 as many times as necessary to cover the bottom of the box with as many different ocean features as possible. Include these features: continental slope, island, guyot, ridge, rift valley, trench, and abyssal plain.

NOTE: Make the abyssal plain as flat as possible.

11. Blot the pulp with the sponge to remove excess water.

12. Let the pulp dry by placing the box in a warm place, such as near a window with direct sun, for several days.

13. Pour the flour over the abyss.

Results A three-dimensional model of the features of the ocean floor is produced.

Why? The top of the box marks the surface of the ocean. The only structure extending above the surface (top of the box) is the island. The flour represents the ooze deposits characteristic of the abyss. **Ooze deposits** are sediment consisting of dust particles from space, volcanic ash, dust blown seaward by winds, and particles of dead organisms that drift down from the upper levels of water. The average depth of ooze is about 2,000 feet (600 m) in the Atlantic Ocean and 1,000 feet (300 m) in the Pacific Ocean.

Solutions to Exercises

1a. *Think!*

- What is the name of a narrow, deep, V-shaped valley in the ocean floor?

  Feature A is a trench.

b. *Think!*

- What is the name of a mountain range rising from the ocean floor?

  Feature B is a ridge.

c. *Think!*

- What is the name of a central valley in a ridge?

  Feature C is a rift valley.

2a. *Think!*

- What is the name of a seamount with a flat top? A guyot.
- Both figures have a flat top, but a guyot does not rise above the ocean's surface.

  Figure B is a guyot.

b. *Think!*

- What is the name of a seamount that extends above the surface of the ocean?

  Figure A is an island.

7
Way Down
Determining the Depth of the Ocean Floor

What You Need to Know

Because the ocean floor is covered with water, it is difficult to study its features. It is easier for scientists to study the surface of the moon, which is at a distance of 238,000 miles (380,800 km), than to map the bottom of the ocean, which has an average depth of about 3 miles (4.8 km). Mapping the ocean floor requires methods different from those used on land.

Scientists usually use sonar to map the ocean floor. Sound waves travel in a straight path through the water and bounce back when they hit an object, which can be the ocean floor or a sunken ship. The time it takes the sound to make the round trip is called the echo time. Sound waves travel in water at a speed of about 5,000 feet (1.5 km) per second. Since half the trip is a return trip, the distance to the ocean floor can be calculated by multiplying the speed of sound through water by the echo time and dividing this product by 2. The depth formula is written as:

$$\text{depth} = (\text{speed of sound} \times \text{echo time}) \div 2$$

Let's Think It Through

1. If the echo time taken from the ocean's surface to the top of the guyot in the side view on the next page is 2 seconds, what is the depth to the top of the guyot? Use the depth formula to calculate the depth of the top of the guyot in kilometers.

2. Use the depth of the top of the guyot in question 1 to determine the scale for the chart in kilometers.

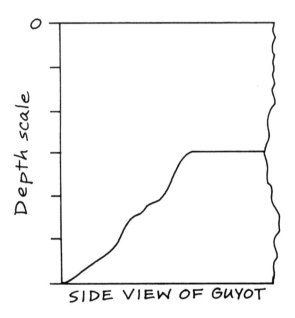

SIDE VIEW OF GUYOT

Answers

1. *Think!*

- The speed of sound in kilometers is 1.5 km per second.
- The echo time from the top of the guyot is 2 seconds.
- The depth is one-half the product of the speed of sound and the echo time.

depth in km $=$ $(1.5 \text{ km} \times 2) \div 2$
$1.5 \text{ km} \times 2$ $=$ 3 km
$3 \text{ km} \div 2$ $=$?

The depth of the top of the guyot is 1.5 km.

2. *Think!*

- The top of the guyot aligns with the third mark below zero on the scale.

- Each scale division is equal to one-third the depth of the top of the guyot, or the depth divided by three.

    1.5 km ÷ 3 = ?

    Each scale division is equal to 0.5 km.

Exercises

1. Echo time taken from location A in the side view of the ocean floor is 4 seconds. Use the depth formula to calculate the depth at location A.

2. Study the side view of the ocean floor, then use the depth at location A to determine the depth at location B. *Hint:* First determine the scale for the chart, then use the scale to determine location B's depth.

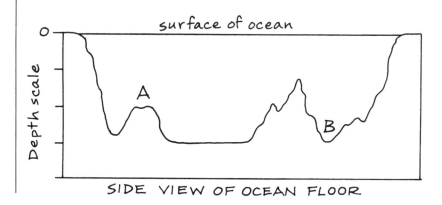

SIDE VIEW OF OCEAN FLOOR

Activity: **SIDE VIEW**

Purpose To map a side view of a model of the ocean floor.

Materials 2 identical chairs with backs at least 30 inches (75 cm) tall
scissors
ruler
string
black marking pen
4 or more books
stool
large pot
large plastic bowl
washer

Procedure

1. Position the chairs 4 feet (1.2 m) apart, with their backs facing each other. The top of each chair back represents the shoreline.

2. Cut a 5-foot (1.5-m) length of string.

3. Tie one end of the string to the back of each chair. The string should be tied at the same height on each chair and stretched taut so that its length is 4 feet (1.2 m). This string represents the surface of the ocean and will be called the surface string.

4. Use the pen to mark off 3-inch (7.5-cm) intervals along the surface string.

5. Position the books, stool, and upturned pot and bowl under the string. These objects and the floor represent the ocean floor.

6. Cut a second piece of string 12 inches (30 cm) longer than the height of the chairs.

7. Tie one end of the second string to the washer.

8. Use the pen to mark off a 1-inch (2.5-cm) scale along the second string. This string will be called the scale.

9. Holding the free end of the scale, position it against the surface string and next to the back of one chair (this is the 0-inch, or 0-cm, mark) and slowly lower the scale until the washer touches an object or the floor.

10. Use the marks on the scale to determine the depth of the ocean. Round off the measurement to the nearest scale marking.

11. Measure the depth of the ocean every 3 inches (7.5 cm) across the length of the surface string, and record the measurement in a data chart like the one shown on the next page.

Data Chart

Distance from Shoreline	Depth
0 inch (0.0 cm)	30 inches (75 cm)
3 inches (7.5 cm)	30 inches (75 cm)
6 inches (15 cm)	23 inches (58 cm)

12. Use your data chart to make a graph of your measurements like the one shown.

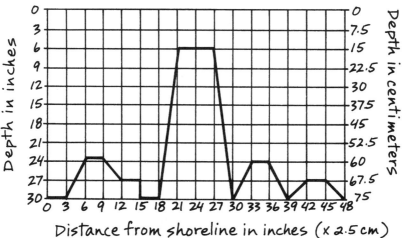

SIDE VIEW OF MODEL

Distance from shoreline in inches (x 2.5 cm)

Results A graph showing the jagged side view of the model of the ocean floor is produced.

Why? Measuring every point on the ocean floor would be difficult. Instead, scientists measure the depth at many different places, as you did in this activity, and combine all the information about the depths into a side view of the ocean floor.

Lowering the scale along the surface string represents taking sonar readings at different distances from the shoreline. The side view made from depth readings, regardless of the method, is jagged because the depth is measured only at intervals instead of along a continuous line. The more measurements taken, the more accurate the side views.

Methods other than sonar are used to study the ocean floor. Underwater laboratories enable scientists to study the ocean floor at close range, but photos taken from space provide the most accurate way of mapping the ocean floor. Different colors on the photos indicate different depths of the ocean.

Solutions to Exercises

1. *Think!*

   - The echo time at location A is 4 seconds.

   - The depth is one-half the product of the speed of sound and the echo time.

     depth in km = $(1.5 \text{ km} \times 4) \div 2$
     $1.5 \text{ km} \times 4 = 6$
     $6 \text{ km} \div 2 = ?$

     At location A, the depth is 3 km.

2. *Think!*

   - Location A aligns with the second mark below zero on the scale.

   - Each scale division is equal to the depth of location A divided by 2.

     $3 \text{ km} \div 2 = 1.5 \text{ km}$

   - The depth of location B, at the third mark, is 3×1.5 km.

     At location B, the depth is 4.5 km.

8
Flowing
The Production and Direction of Currents

What You Need to Know

Air (a mixture of gases, made mostly of nitrogen and oxygen) surrounds the earth. This blanket of air is known as the earth's **atmosphere.** The temperature of the earth's atmosphere is warmest above an area near the **tropics** (the area of the earth that is closest to the equator) that extends from about 30°N to 30°S and coolest above the **polar regions** (areas between 60° and 90°N and between 60° and 90°S). A basic scientific rule regarding **fluids** (gases or liquids) is that warm fluids rise and cold fluids sink. The hot air at the equator rises, then moves toward the poles, where it cools and sinks back to the earth. When the hot air rises, the sinking colder air rushes in to take its place. This up-and-down movement of air due to temperature differences is called **convection currents,** and the generally horizontal movement of air is called **wind.**

The major wind patterns on the earth are called **prevailing winds.** The direction of these winds is generally determined by three things: (1) convection currents; (2) the earth's rotation from west to east; and (3) **air pressure** (the force air puts on an area). Air pressure is of two types: **highs** (areas of the atmosphere with higher air pressure than surrounding areas) and **lows** (areas of the atmosphere with lower air pressure than surrounding areas). Diagram A shows the direction winds would be if only convection currents caused wind. Diagram B shows winds produced as a result of the combination of convection currents and the earth's rotation. Diagram C shows what happens to winds as the result of all three factors: convection currents, the earth's rotation, and air pressure.

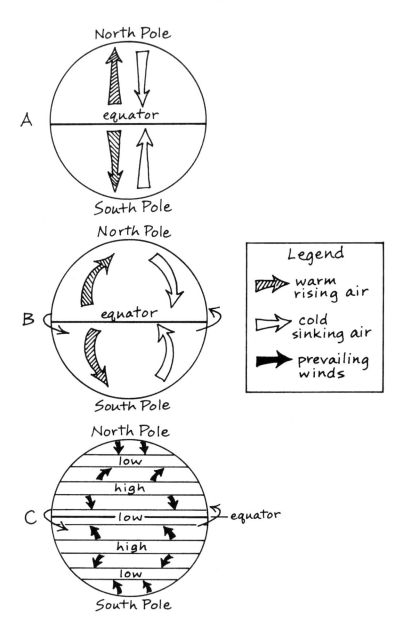

A **surface current** is an ocean current that is caused by wind. Prevailing winds have the greatest effect on surface currents. These currents are usually the same year after year, with warmer currents moving away from the equator and cooler currents moving toward the equator. Because of prevailing winds, rotation of the earth, and the position of the continents, surface currents move in a large, mainly circular pattern. This circular pattern is generally like the wind patterns above the water: in a clockwise direction in the Northern Hemisphere and counterclockwise in the Southern Hemisphere.

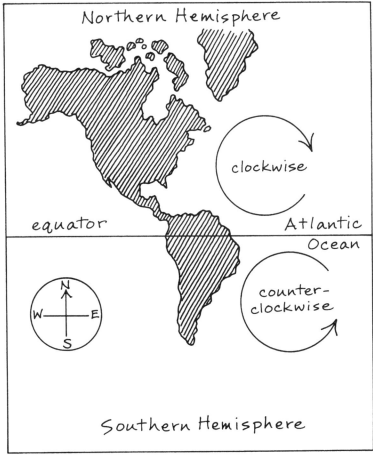

DIRECTION OF SURFACE CURRENT FLOW

Let's Think It Through

Study the map and choose the figure, A or B, that shows the direction of the surface current flow for each of these currents:

1. North Equatorial Current

2. South Equatorial Current

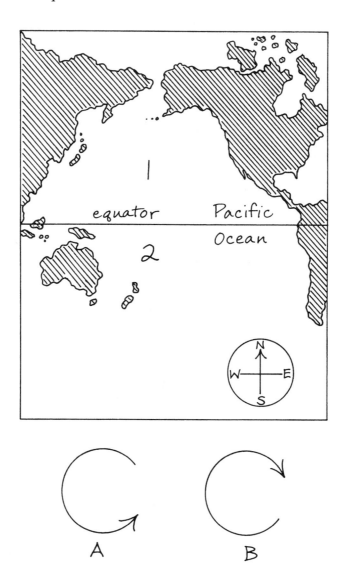

Answers

1. *Think!*

- The Northern Hemisphere is the region above the equator.
- Surface currents generally move in a clockwise direction in the Northern Hemisphere.

  Figure B shows the clockwise current flow for the North Equatorial Current.

2. *Think!*

- The Southern Hemisphere is the region below the equator.
- Surface currents generally move in a counterclockwise pattern in the Southern Hemisphere.

  Figure A shows the counterclockwise current flow for the South Equatorial Current.

Exercises

Use the Ocean Currents map on the next page to answer the following questions:

1. Is the Gulf Stream a warm or cold current?

2. Which coastline of South America should have a warmer current, the west or the east?

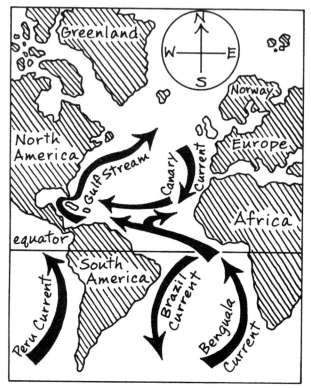

OCEAN CURRENTS

Activity: DEFLECTED

Purpose To determine how the rotation of the earth affects the direction of the ocean currents.

Materials sheet of typing paper
ruler
pencil
transparent tape
coffee can or other can of comparable size
duct tape
felt-tip pen
helper

Procedure

1. Fold the paper in half lengthwise.

2. Open the paper and, with the ruler and pencil, draw a line along the fold.

3. Turn the paper so that the line runs from left to right, then label the line Equator. Print 30°N at the top right edge and 30°S at the bottom right edge of the paper as shown.

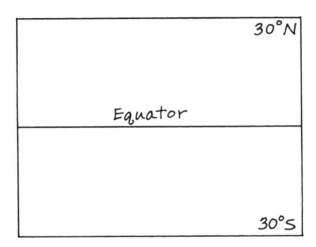

4. Refold the paper and use transparent tape to secure it to the can so that the N shows at the top.

5. Stand the can on a table, next to the edge and near a corner.

6. Press the ruler against the edge of the table so that the top of the ruler is even with the top of the can.

7. Use duct tape to secure the ruler to the edge of the table.

8. Rotate the can so that about 1 inch (2.5 cm) of the right end of the paper extends past the right edge of the ruler.

9. Hold the pen against the top of the paper and next to the right edge of the ruler.

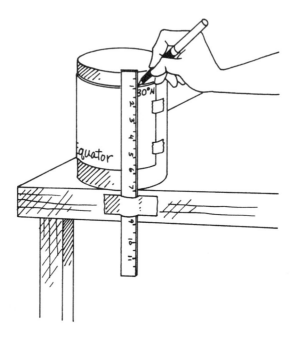

10. Ask your helper to turn the can quickly in a counterclockwise direction about one quarter turn while you draw a line on the paper straight down the edge of the ruler.

11. Draw an arrowhead at the end of this line.

12. Remove the paper from the can, turn the paper over, and tape it to the can again with the S showing at the bottom.

13. Return the can to its original position on the table, then repeat step 8.

14. Hold the pen against the *bottom* of the paper and next to the right edge of the ruler.

15. Again, ask your helper to rotate the can counterclockwise as you draw a line on the paper straight *up* the edge of the ruler.

16. Draw an arrowhead at the end of this line.

17. Remove the paper from the can and unfold it.

18. Observe the direction of the two arrows.

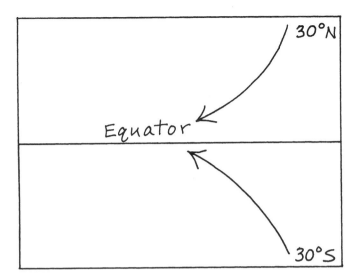

Results   Both arrows curve to the left and toward the equator.

Why?   Prevailing winds drive the ocean waters before them, creating surface currents. These wind patterns, and consequently the surface currents they create, would flow only in a north or south direction were it not for the rotation of the earth. But the earth's rotation causes ocean currents to **deflect** (bend) even more than it deflects air currents. This deflection of fluids as a result of the earth's rotation is called the **Coriolis effect.** In this activity, turning the can represents the rotation of the earth. The lines you drew along the ruler would have been straight up and down if the can had not been turned.

Imagine you are standing at the equator on the Coriolis Effect diagram. If you look toward the North Pole, your right hand points east, just as currents moving north from the equator are deflected to the east. If you stand at the North Pole and face the equator, your right hand points west, just as currents moving south from the North Pole are deflected to the west. You can use this same mental exercise of facing in the direction of the current and pointing with your *left* hand to reason out the east or west direction of currents in the Southern Hemisphere.

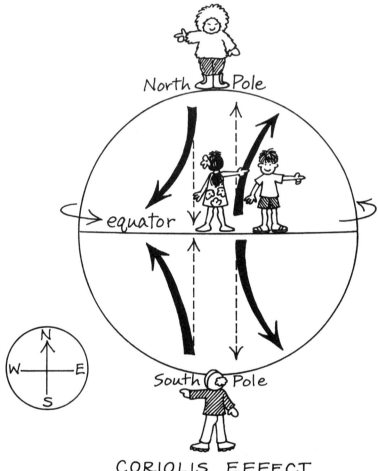

CORIOLIS EFFECT

Solutions to Exercises

1. *Think!*

- The Gulf Stream starts near the equator and moves in a general northward direction away from the equator.
- Currents moving away from the equator are warm.

  The Gulf Stream is a warm current.

2. *Think!*

- The Peru Current on the west coast of South America flows toward the equator, thus it is a cooler current than the east coast's Brazil Current, which flows away from the equator.

  The east coast of South America should have a warmer current.

9
Up and Down
Learning About Water Waves

What You Need to Know

Many of us have played in the waves at the seashore, but have you ever wondered why waves happen? **Water waves** are a disturbance on the surface of water that repeats itself. Most waves are caused by the wind blowing across the surface of the water. First, small ripples form, and then larger ripples may form and grow into larger and larger waves. Both ripples and waves move across the surface of the water, but the water itself does not travel with the waves, but moves up and down instead. Water waves behave in a similar manner to waves moving through a rope. In the diagram, the rope moves up and down as the

waves move forward, but the rope does not move forward with the waves. Likewise, waves pass through water but do not carry the water with them.

As a wave travels through deep water, each water particle moves up and down in a circular motion, ending up nearly in the same position as where it started. In shallow water, near the shore, the water particle no longer moves in a circle. As the water particles in the **trough** (the low point of the wave) hit against the land at the shoreline, **friction** (the force that slows the motion of two things that touch each other) slows their motion, but the particles in the high point of the wave, called the **crest,** are not slowed. This results in a **breaker,** which is a wave whose crest falls forward and crashes into the trough.

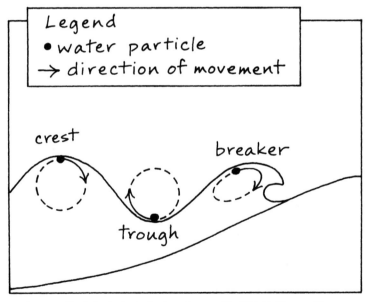

MOVEMENT OF A WATER PARTICLE

The horizontal, or left-to-right, distance between similar points of two waves in a row is called the **wavelength.** In other words, wavelength is the distance from one wave's crest to the next or from one wave's trough to the next. Generally, the wavelength of ocean waves varies from a few yards (meters) to a few hundred yards (meters). The vertical, or top-to-bottom, distance between the crest and trough of a wave is its **wave height.** Wave height depends on the speed of the wind blowing across the water's surface, the amount of open water present, and the duration of the wind. An increase in any one of these can cause an increase in wave height.

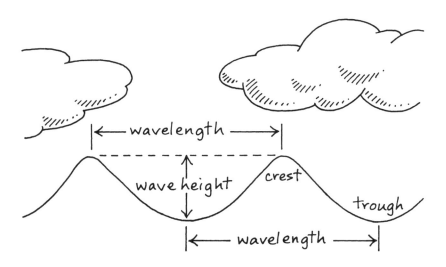

While wind causes most ocean waves, underwater disturbances such as volcanoes, earthquakes, or landslides can cause freakishly long, high-speed waves called **tsunamis.** The speed and wavelength of tsunamis across the open ocean is tremendous. Wavelengths can be as great as 100 miles (160 km), with forward wave speeds of up to 500 miles per hour (800 kph). In the open ocean, the height of these waves may be only 12 inches (30 cm). But, as the waves approach land, they can build up to heights of 50 feet (15 m) or more. Because the wavelength of tsunamis is so long, about 15 minutes can pass between the time one destructive wave hits the shore and the next wave arrives.

Oceanographer's Toolbox: WAVE VIEWER

Materials scissors
ruler
two 3-by-5-inch (7.5-by-12.5-cm) index cards
transparent tape
colored, transparent, plastic report folder
black marking pen

Procedure

1. Cut a 2-by-2-inch (5-by-5-cm) window in the middle of one of the long sides of one index card.

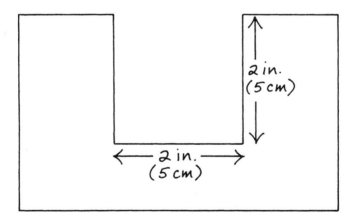

2. Place the cut card on top of the second index card.

3. Secure the two cards together with tape only on the long sides. These connected cards will be called the wave viewer.

4. Cut a 3-by-11-inch (7.5-by-27.5-cm) strip from the plastic folder.

5. Lay the plastic strip over the diagram of the wave so that the top left corner of the strip is in the corner formed by the dashed lines.

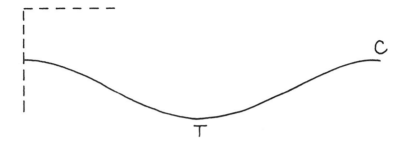

6. Trace the wave, marking the letters on the plastic. C marks the wave's crest and T marks its trough.

7. Move the plastic to the left until the right end of the wave traced on the plastic touches the left end of the wave in the diagram. Make sure that the top of the plastic is lined up with the horizontal dashed line, then repeat step 6.

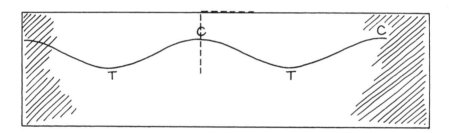

8. Cut a 2-by-4-inch (5-by-10-cm) piece from the plastic folder.

9. Lay the plastic piece over the diagram and trace the circle, dots, and arrows.

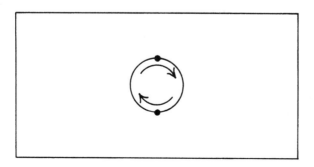

10. Insert the right short end of the long plastic strip in the wave viewer.

11. Move the strip so that the crest of a wave (the letter C dot) is centered between the right and left sides of the window in the wave viewer.

12. Lay the plastic with the circle over the wave viewer's window and position it so that the top dot on the circle touches the center of the wave's crest (the part of the wave below the letter C).

13. Tape the piece of plastic with the circle to the wave viewer.

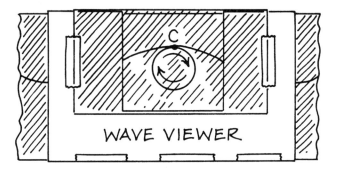

WAVE VIEWER

Let's Think It Through

Use your wave viewer to determine the motion of a water particle. Follow these steps:

1. Lay the wave viewer on a table.

2. Hold the wave viewer in place with your right hand while you slowly push the plastic strip through the holder with your left hand.

3. Observe the direction of the arrow where the dots on the circumference of the circle touch the wave. The dots on the circle represent the water particle at the crest (top dot) and at the trough (bottom dot).

Answer

Think!

- When the crest passes, the water particle moves forward in the same direction as the wave is traveling.

- When the trough passes, the water particle moves backward.

  The water particle moves through a complete circle and returns to approximately the original spot.

Exercises

Use your wave viewer and figures A and B to answer the following questions:

1. Name the part of the wave where the water particles are located in each figure.

2. Is the water particle in figure A about to move down or up?

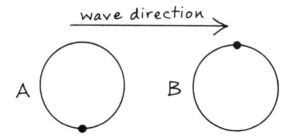

Activity: BOBBER

Purpose To determine if surface water moves with each wave.

Materials large, rectangular, glass baking dish
tap water
scissors

drinking straw
timer
unsharpened pencil

Procedure

1. Fill the baking dish three-fourths full with water.

2. Cut about 1 inch (2.5 cm) from one end of the straw.

3. Place the small piece of straw in the center of the water in the dish.

4. Wait about 30 seconds to allow the water to become calm.

5. With the unsharpened end of the pencil, tap the surface of the water at one end of the dish.

6. Observe the straw and the surface of the water.

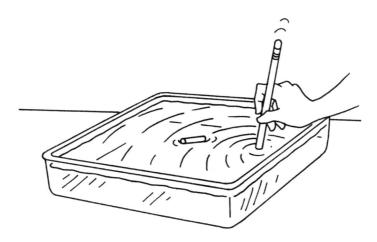

Results Waves start where the water is touched by the pencil, move to the opposite end of the dish, and return again. This back-and-forth movement of the waves may happen several times. While the waves are moving back and forth across the surface, the straw is moving up and down.

Why? Waves are a transfer of energy from one water **molecule** (the smallest particle of a substance that retains all the properties of that substance) to the next. As the energy of a water wave moves forward, the water moves up and down, but there is only a slight horizontal movement of the water molecules. In one complete wavelength, a molecule of water moves through a complete circular path and ends up at about the same place that it started. Thus, objects floating on the water's surface may move horizontally slightly, but mostly they bob up and down as waves pass through the water.

Solutions to Exercises

1. *Think!*

- What part of the wave is passing when the water particle is at the bottom of its cycle?

  The water particle in figure A is located in the trough of the wave.

Think!

- What part of the wave is passing when the water particle is at the top of its cycle?

  The water particle in figure B is located in the crest of the wave.

2. *Think!*

- Water particles in a wave's trough move backward from the direction the wave is traveling.

  The particle in figure A is about to move up.

10
Wash Out

Learning How Waves Change Shorelines

What You Need to Know

The land at the shoreline is called the **shore.** There are different kinds of shores. Some shores have **beaches** (smooth, sloping stretches of sand and pebbles) and some do not. Beaches vary in width and in the size of rock material. Some are narrow and some are wide. Narrow beaches may be less than 3 feet (1 m) wide, while some wider beaches are over 300 feet (90 m) wide. The material on a beach is usually thought to be fine sand, but some are covered with pebbles or even rock. The width of a beach and the size of its material are determined by the age of the beach. Generally, young beaches are narrow and have larger particles, while older beaches are wider with smaller particles.

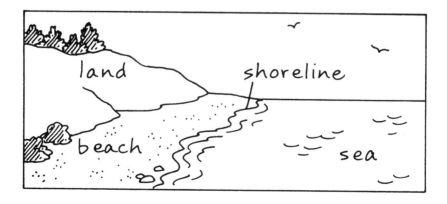

The color of a beach depends on the kind of rock that is exposed along the shore. White beaches, like those in the Bahama Islands, are made of limestone, which is a white rock. This lime sand is often called "coral sand" even though it may not come from deposits of these marine animals. Sandy beaches, along most of the shores in the United States, are made of grains of either granite or sandstone, which are light-colored rocks. Some of the Hawaiian Islands have black beaches that are formed from the **erosion** (the process by which materials of the earth's surface are slowly worn away) of a dark volcanic rock called basalt.

Some of the loose material on beaches is brought and deposited by rivers, while some is the result of erosion of rock on the shore by wave action. While moving water alone can wear away large rocks over a period of time, often waves contain small pieces of sand or rock that act to speed up erosion. This is because the particles carried in the water rub and pound against the rock. This is like rubbing a nail file back and forth across a fingernail. The rough particles on the file, like the small pieces of sand or rock in the water, wear away the surface they rub against.

Rocky **headlands** (projections of land that extend into deep water), such as steep cliffs, take the place of beaches along some shorelines. As waves approach the land, they hit the headland first, since it juts out into the sea from the land. Fast, energetic waves lose energy and slow down when they slam into a headland. The slower moving wave is then deflected toward the shore. As waves continue to hit against the rocky surfaces of the headland, rock pieces are eroded. Part of the result of erosion of rocky headlands is the production of tiny pebbles and sand particles. If the shore has a steep slope, the sand and pebbles are washed back to sea, but if the shore has a gentle slope, the particles can build up. Thus, shorelines with sand usually have gentle slopes toward the sea.

The particles eroded from rocky headlands are carried in and help wear away the headlands to form sea cliffs, sea caves, sea arches, and sea stacks. As waves pound against a headland, small pieces as well as large slabs of rock are broken away, forming a vertical rock wall that goes down sharply to the sea, called a **sea cliff.** In time, soft rock in some cliffs is washed away by waves. These hollowed-out places in sea cliffs are called **sea caves.** Continued erosion of rock can wash away the walls of a sea cave, creating a hole in the headland. This produces a stone bridge-like structure called a **sea arch,** which extends above the sea, connecting a rock column in the sea with a sea cliff. If the top of the arch is washed away, the column of rock standing in the sea near the shore is called a **sea stack.**

Let's Think It Through

1. Identify the rock structures in the diagram.

2. List the rock structures in the order in which they most likely were formed.

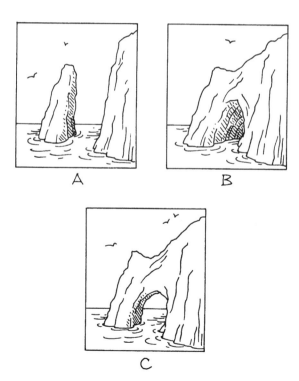

Answers

1. *Think!*

   • What is the name of a column of rock standing in the sea near a shore?

   Structure A is a sea stack.

   Think!

   • What is the name of a hollowed-out place in a sea cliff?

   Structure B is a sea cave.

   Think!

   • What is the name of a stone bridge-like structure that extends above the sea, connecting a rock column in the sea with a sea cliff?

   Structure C is a sea arch.

2. *Think!*

   • A sea cave (B) forms when waves wash away soft rock from a sea cliff.

   • A sea arch (C) forms when waves wash away the walls of a sea cave.

   • A sea stack (A) forms when waves wash away the top of a sea arch.

   The rock structures most likely were formed in this order: sea cave, sea arch, sea stack.

Exercises

1. Study the figures to determine which is most likely the older beach.

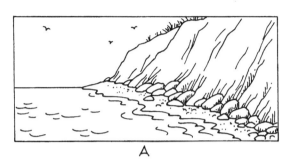

A

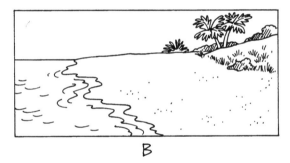

B

2. Study the diagram to determine which part of the shore is eroded at a slower rate, where wave A hits or where wave B hits.

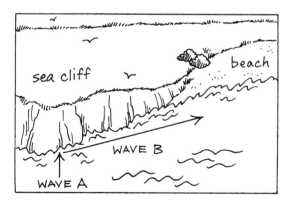

Activity: WASH OUT

Purpose   To simulate the effect of headlands on wave action.

Materials   paint-roller pan
5 cups (1,250 ml) sand
2 quarts (2 liters) tap water
pencil
2 cups (500 ml) gravel

Procedure

1. Cover the bottom of the pan with 4 cups (1,000 ml) of the sand, building up a small "beach" at the shallow end.

2. Pour the water into the deep end of the pan.

3. Make a mental note of the appearance of the sandy beach in the pan.

4. Make waves by laying the pencil in the deep end of the pan and quickly moving the pencil up and down with your fingertips.

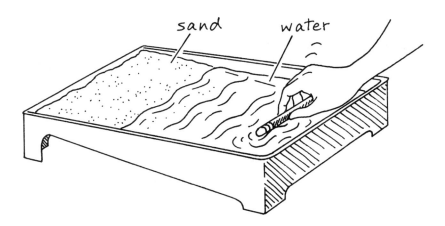

5. Mound the gravel in the center of the shoreline.

6. Pour the remaining 1 cup (250 ml) of sand on the beach to replace all or part of the sand washed away.

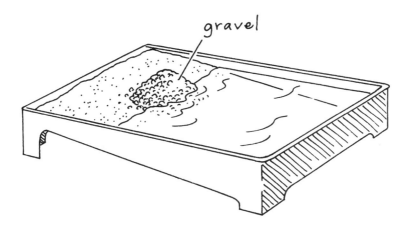

gravel

7. Make waves with the pencil as in step 4.

Results Without the gravel, more sand is washed from the beach. With the gravel, very little beach sand is washed away, but part of the gravel is.

Why? Without the gravel, the waves hit the sandy beach, moving some of the sand down into the water. With the gravel, fewer waves hit the beach and less sand is washed away. With the gravel in place, some of the waves hit the beach, but many are deflected back toward the deep end of the pan. Since the pan is small, these waves bounce off the pan's wall and return toward the shore again. These deflected waves lose energy every time they change direction, so even if they hit the beach instead of the gravel, they do not move much of the sand.

The mound of gravel is a model of a headland. Waves wear these projections down faster than adjacent inland beaches. This is because waves that hit a headland have more energy. The faster a wave moves, the more energy it has. When waves hit a headland, their speed is decreased. Some of the waves swing around the headland and continue on toward the beach at a slower speed, while some of the waves strike the headland head-on and are deflected in different directions.

Solutions to Exercises

1. *Think!*

- Generally, the smaller the particles on a beach, the older the beach.

- Sand grains are much smaller than pebbles.

  Figure B, with the sandy beach, is most likely the older of the two beaches.

2. *Think!*

- Fast, energetic waves hit headlands, such as steep cliffs that jut out into the sea from the land, first.

- Waves decrease in speed when they collide with headlands and are deflected toward the shore.

- Slow moving waves have less energy than fast moving waves and erode the land at a slower rate.

  Wave B is slower and has less energy than wave A, thus the beach where wave B hits is eroded more slowly than the face of the sea cliff.

11
Bulge

Learning about Tides

What You Need to Know

Tides (the regular rise and fall of the ocean's surface) are waves caused by the **gravity** (the force that pulls objects on or near a heavenly body, such as a planet, moon, or star, toward the center of the heavenly body) of the moon and sun. The diagram shows how the moon's gravitational pull on the earth produces tides. Note the large bulge on the side of the earth facing the moon. This shows that the moon is pulling on the ocean's surface, causing it to rise. A second bulge appears on the side of the earth that faces away from the moon. This happens partly because the moon pulls more strongly on the **lithosphere** (the solid part of the earth) than it does on the water on that side. Because the water is not attached to the lithosphere, the water is left behind. Both bulges include water that is drawn from the area of ocean between the bulges. In these areas, the ocean's surface falls.

Rising of the ocean's surface is called **high tide** or **flood tide,** and falling of the ocean's surface is called **low tide** or **ebb tide.** High and low tides occur during each 24-hour day. If the moon remained stationary during the 24 hours of the earth's rotation, the times for high and low tides would not change from day to day. But the moon is not stationary; it rotates around the earth. During the 24 hours that the earth is revolving, the moon's rotation takes it slightly past the position from which the earth started turning. This produces a 24½-hour tidal cycle and results in the time of tides changing from day to day.

The sun also has an effect on tides, though the effect is smaller than that of the moon because of its great distance from the earth. This effect is more noticeable when the sun, moon, and earth are in line with each other. In this position, the high tides are higher than normal and the low tides are lower than normal. Although these tides are called **spring tides,** they have nothing to do with the season. *Spring* is from a Saxon word meaning "to swell." Spring tides occur two times each month, during the new moon and full moon positions as shown.

The lowest tides occur when the sun and moon are at right angles to each other. The gravity of each is pulling the ocean

water in different directions. In this position, there is little difference between the depth at high and low tide. These tides are
called **neap tides.** *Neap* is from a Saxon word meaning "scarce,
or lacking." These tides also occur twice a month, during the
first and third quarter phases of the moon.

Let's Think It Through

Study the diagram and identify the location(s)—A, B, C, or
D—with the highest tides.

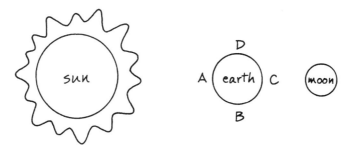

Answer

Think!

- The gravity of the sun and moon pull on the earth, producing tides.
- The highest tides occur when the sun and moon are in line with the earth.

Locations A and C have the highest tides.

Exercises

Study the diagram to answer the following questions:

1. Which position(s) of the moon—A, B, C, or D—produce neap tides?

2. Which position(s) of the moon produce spring tides?

Activity: BULGES

Purpose To make a model representing high and low tides.

Materials 18-inch (45-cm) piece of 18-gauge insulated wire
duct tape
shallow cardboard box

pencil
drawing compass
typing paper
scissors
marking pen
8-inch (20-cm) piece of string
ruler
transparent tape
quarter

Procedure

1. Bend the wire into a circle and connect the ends with duct tape.

2. Turn the box upside down.

3. Push the point of the pencil into the bottom and near one edge of the box so that the pencil stands vertically as in the diagram on the next page.

4. Place the wire circle over the pencil and on the box so that the wire touches the side of the pencil.

5. Use the compass to draw a 4-inch (10-cm) -diameter circle on the paper.

6. Cut out the circle and write Earth across its center.

7. Tie the center of the string around the wire circle at a point directly across from the pencil.

8. Measure and cut both ends of the string so that the pieces of string on the wire are 3 inches (7.5 cm) long.

9. Tape one end of the string to the center of the paper circle.

10. Tape the other end of the string to the quarter.

11. Position the paper circle in the center of the wire circle. The string attached to the paper will be loose.

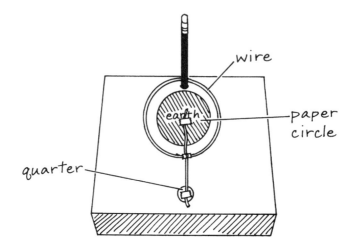

12. Slowly pull the quarter in a direction away from the pencil until the string attached to the paper circle is straight.

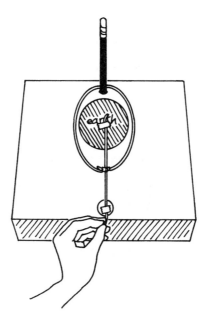

13. Observe the shape of the wire around the paper circle.

Results The wire is pulled into an oval shape, with one of its pointed ends directed toward the quarter.

Why? The model made in this activity includes the earth's lithosphere, represented by the paper circle, with its oceans, represented by the wire circle, and the moon, represented by the quarter. The string represents the moon's gravitational pull. Pulling the quarter demonstrates the effect of the moon's gravitational pull on the ocean's surface and the earth's lithosphere. This pull results in a buildup of water on the side of the earth facing the moon (the quarter) as well as on the side of the earth opposite the moon, causing high and low tides. Although the model shows the shape of the ocean's surface as a result of the moon's gravitational pull, it exaggerates the movement of the earth's lithosphere (the paper circle) in comparison to the movement of the ocean's surface. It also seems to show that water completely covers the earth's lithosphere, which is not true.

Solutions to Exercises

1. *Think!*

- Neap tides are the lowest tides.
- The lowest tides are produced when the sun and moon are at right angles to each other.

  Moon positions B and D produce neap tides.

2. *Think!*

- Spring tides are the highest tides.
- The highest tides are produced when the sun, moon, and earth are in line with each other.

  Moon positions A and C produce spring tides.

12
Hot and Cold

Comparing the Differences in Temperature in Different Parts of the Ocean

What You Need to Know

The temperature of **seawater** (water from the ocean) varies from place to place and changes with the seasons. Surface temperatures can vary greatly at different locations, but at great depths there is little difference in temperature. Surface temperatures are usually between 32°F (0°C) and 86°F (30°C). However, there are warmer and colder areas. Warmer areas occur at low latitudes and colder areas at high latitudes, because the sun's rays strike the earth most directly at the equator and least directly at the poles.

At the poles, the water can become so cold that it freezes. The **freezing point** (temperature at which a liquid changes into a solid) of **freshwater** (water that is not salty) is 32°F (0°C), but seawater freezes at a lower temperature because of the dissolved salts in it. The freezing point of seawater is about 28.6°F (–1.9°C). In the Arctic Ocean, most of the surface water is frozen year-round.

There are generally three temperature layers in the ocean, especially in parts where the water is deep. The temperature of the top layer, called the **surface layer,** changes only slightly with depth. Below the surface layer is a layer of water called the **thermocline.** The temperature in this layer drops rapidly the deeper you go. Under the thermocline is the **cold layer.** Very little sunlight reaches this bottom layer, thus it is colder than the upper layers. The temperature in this layer changes very little with depth.

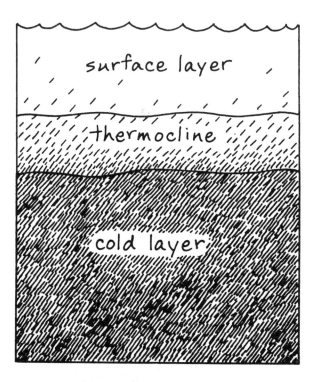

Let's Think It Through

1. Study the Seawater Temperatures chart on the next page to answer the following questions:

  a. What is the surface temperature?

  b. What would be the predicted temperature at 22 m?

Seawater Temperatures

Depth, in Meters	Temperature, in °C
0	25
2	24
4	23
6	21
8	20
10	15
12	8
14	4
16	4
18	4
20	4

2. Use the Latitudes map to determine which boat is most likely sailing in warmer water.

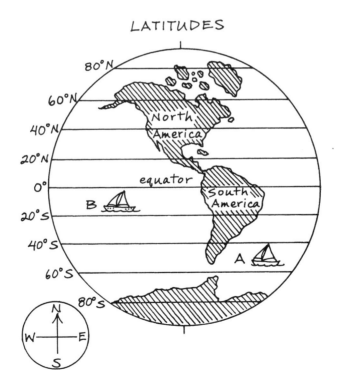

Answers

1a. *Think!*

- The depth at the surface is 0 m, as shown at the top of column 1 in the chart.
- What temperature in column 2 is directly across from the 0 in column 1?

The temperature at the surface is 25 °C.

b. *Think!*

- The temperature at great depths does not change much.
- There is no temperature change between 14 m and 20 m. The temperature at these depths is 4°C.

The temperature at 22 m is most likely 4 °C.

2. *Think!*

- Seawater is warmest at the equator.
- Which boat is closer to the equator?

Boat B, at latitude 22 °S, is sailing in warmer water.

Exercise

Study the graph on the next page to answer the following questions:

1. Between what depths is the thermocline?

2. What is the temperature change between 12 m and 21 m?

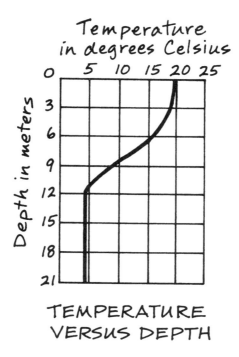

TEMPERATURE VERSUS DEPTH

Activity: CURRENTS

Purpose   To demonstrate the effect that temperature has on the motion of water.

Materials   two 2-liter soda bottles
scissors
masking tape
marking pen
2-quart (2-liter) measuring bowl with pouring
   spout
ice
cold tap water
timer
stiff paper, such as the back of a writing tablet
paper hole-punch
warm tapwater
blue food coloring

one 2-liter soda bottle cap
paper towel
duct tape
spoon
adult helper

Procedure

1. Ask your adult helper to prepare the bottles by following these steps:

   • Remove any plastic cap rings on the neck of the bottles.

   • Cut one of the bottles in half. Keep the top half and throw away the bottom half.

   NOTE: Recycle discarded plastic.

2. Use the masking tape to label the intact bottle A and the top of the cut bottle B.

3. Fill the bowl about one-fourth full with ice, then fill the bowl halfway with cold water. Allow the bowl of water to stand for about 5 minutes.

4. Cut a circle the size of the mouth of a soda bottle from the stiff paper.

5. Punch two holes in the paper circle with the paper hole-punch.

6. Fill bottle A with warm water.

7. Add food coloring to the water to produce a dark blue liquid. Place the cap on the bottle and rotate the bottle back and forth to mix the water and coloring thoroughly.

8. Remove the lid and dry the mouth of the bottle with the paper towel.

9. Place the paper circle over the mouth of bottle A, then place the mouth of bottle B upside down on top of the paper circle.

10. Secure the mouths of the bottles together with duct tape.

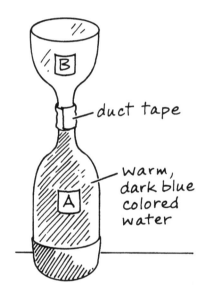

11. Use the spoon to remove any unmelted ice from the bowl, then pour the cold water from the bowl into bottle B.

12. Observe the movement of the colored water.

Results A stream of warm, colored water rises from bottle A into the cold, colorless water of bottle B. The stream of colorless water from bottle B moving down into bottle A may not be visible, but in a short period of time, as the colorless water mixes with the colored water, the color of the water at the top of bottle A is less intense.

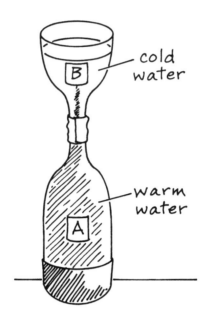

Why? Cold water molecules **contract** (draw closer together), and warm water molecules **expand** (spread farther apart). Thus, there are more molecules in cold water than in an equal volume of warm water, making cold water heavier than warm water. This causes the lighter warm water to rise, and the heavier cold water to sink. The up-and-down movements of water due to differences in temperature are called convection currents. The water in the surface layer of the ocean is well mixed due to convection currents, thus its temperature changes only slightly with depth.

Solutions to Exercises

1. *Think!*

- The thermocline is the zone where the temperature changes the most.

- A straight vertical graph line indicates a change in depth, but no change in temperature.

- An angled graph line indicates a change in both depth and temperature. The greater the angle, the less the change in depth and the greater the change in temperature.

- Between what marks on the depth scale is the graph line at the greatest angle?

  The thermocline on the graph is between 3 m and 12 m.

2. *Think!*

- The graph line is a straight vertical between 12 m and 21 m.

  There is no temperature change between 12 m and 21 m.

13
Squeezed

Factors that Cause Water Pressure

What You Need to Know

Pressure is a force applied over a certain area. Since water has **weight** (measure of the downward force of an object toward the center of the earth due to gravity), it exerts pressure. The amount of pressure exerted by water is determined by two factors. One is the height or depth of the water. As the depth of water increases, the pressure also increases. Water pressure increases equally with depth. In other words, water pressure at a depth of 20 feet (6 m) is twice that at a depth of 10 feet (3 m). The pressure at 30 feet (9 m) is three times that at 10 feet (3 m) and so on. The amount of water present does not affect the pressure. If the salt content is equal, the pressure 12 inches (30 cm) below the surface of the water in a saltwater aquarium is equal to the pressure 12 inches (30 cm) below the surface of the ocean.

The second factor that determines the pressure of water is its density. **Density** is the "heaviness" of an object, based on its **mass** (the amount of material in an object) compared to its volume. As the density of water increases, the pressure that it exerts also increases. The density of seawater is greater than that of water in lakes, rivers, and streams. This is due to the fact that there is a greater amount of salt dissolved in seawater. A diver that is 20 feet (6 m) below the surface of the water in a lake has a column of water 20 feet (6 m) tall above him or her. If this same diver were at the same depth in the ocean, the pressure would be greater. This is because a column of seawater weighs slightly more than an equal-size column of lake water.

Because pressure increases with depth, divers experience physical changes as they descend, or go deeper. At a depth of about 10 feet (3 m), the diver's ears "pop" just as yours do in an airplane, elevator, or anywhere there is a change in the air pressure outside your body. At greater depths, divers have a difficult time seeing because of the pressure on their eyes. This problem is solved by wearing special masks to cover the eyes.

At still greater depths, the higher pressure on the body causes nitrogen, a gas in the air being breathed by the diver, to dissolve in the diver's blood and body fluids. If the diver comes to the surface too quickly, the reduced pressure causes bubbles of nitrogen to form in the fluids. These bubbles cause severe pain and can block various blood vessels in the lungs, brain, and heart. Because of the swelling of the tissue and the pain in bending elbows and other joints, this condition is commonly called the "bends." To prevent the bends, divers make the ascent, or return to the surface, from great depths very slowly so that the nitrogen gradually leaves the body fluids as the pressure gradually decreases.

Let's Think It Through

The gauges outside the aquarium in the diagram indicate water pressure at the surface, middle, and bottom of the water. Study the diagram and answer these questions:

1. Where is the pressure the greatest?

2. Draw a gauge showing the pressure at 1 m.

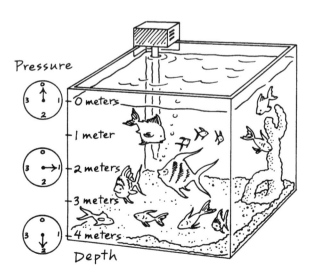

Answers

1. *Think!*

- The pressure gauge showing the highest pressure is at what depth?

  The pressure is greatest at 4 m, which is at the bottom of the aquarium.

2. *Think!*

- Pressure increases equally for each meter of depth.
- There is one unit of pressure at a depth of 2 m.
- The pressure at a depth of 1 m will be half as great as the pressure at 2 m.

  The gauge showing the pressure at 1 m is:

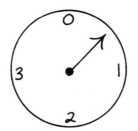

PRESSURE GAUGE

Exercises

Study the diagram to answer these questions:

1. Which diver has the least amount of water pressure on his body?

2. If diver B at a depth of 3 m has two units of pressure on his body, what is the pressure on diver D at a depth of 6 m?

3. Which diver represents the depth at which "popping" of the ears is experienced due to pressure changes?

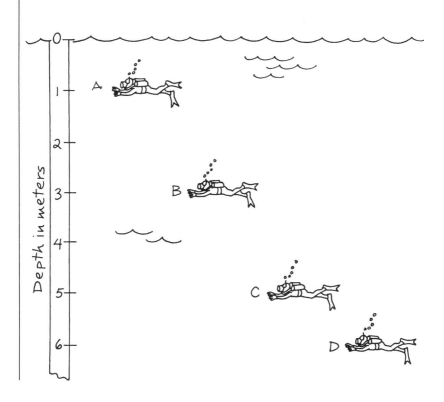

Activity: SQUIRTER

Purpose   To compare the pressure of water at different depths.

Materials   pencil
7-ounce (210-ml) paper cup
masking tape
quart (liter) pitcher
tap water
helper
adult helper

Procedure

1. Ask an adult to use the pencil to punch three holes of similar diameter on a slightly diagonal line, at the top, middle, and bottom of the cup.

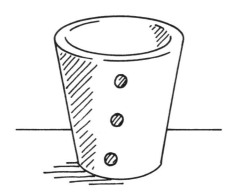

2. Place a strip of masking tape over the holes on the outside of the cup.

3. Set the cup on the edge of a sink.

4. Fill the pitcher and cup with water.

5. Remove the tape from the cup, and ask your helper to keep the cup filled by pouring water from the pitcher into the cup.

6. Observe the distance each stream of water squirts.

Results   The squirting distance of the streams increases from top to bottom.

Why?   Water pressure increases with depth because of the weight of the water pushing down from above. The greater the pressure, the farther the steam of water squirts, so the stream of water coming from the bottom hole goes the farthest.

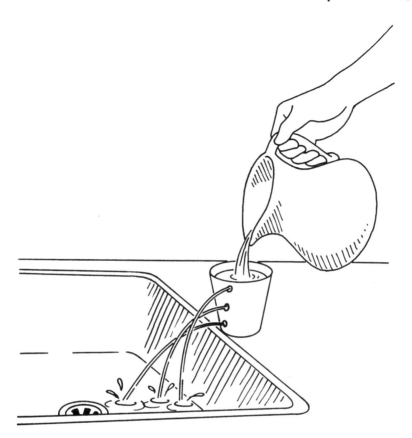

Solutions to Exercises

1. *Think!*

- Water pressure increases with depth.
- Which diver is at the least depth?

  Diver A has the least amount of pressure on his body.

2. *Think!*

- Water pressure increases equally with depth.

- Diver D is at depth equal to two times that of diver B, thus the pressure on diver D will be two times that of diver B.

- The pressure on diver B is two units.

  The pressure on diver D is four units.

3. *Think!*

- Divers' ears "pop" at about 3 m.

- Which diver is swimming at a depth at or near 3 m?

  Diver B's ears are "popping."

14
Salty

Why the Ocean Is Salty

What You Need to Know

Seawater tastes salty because of the salts dissolved in it. A mixture of 1 tablespoon (15 ml) of table salt in 1 quart (1 liter) of water contains about the same amount of salt as does seawater. Sodium chloride is the chemical name for the salt known as table salt. This salt is the most abundant salt in seawater. However, there are seven common salts in seawater. The names of these salts and the percentage of each that is found in any seawater sample is shown in the pie chart on the next page. The percentage of a particular salt in seawater is generally the same. This means that no matter how much salt is dissolved in a sample of seawater, about 77.75 percent of the salt is sodium chloride and the percentages of the other salts also generally stay the same.

Salinity is the measure of the amount of salt dissolved in a liquid. The average salinity of seawater is 35 parts per thousand. This is written as 35 ppt. This means that 35 units of salt are in every 1,000 units of seawater. The gram is the unit most commonly used in measuring salinity, but any mass or weight unit, such as pounds, can be used. While most samples of seawater have a salinity of 35 ppt, it does vary from place to place. The range of salinity of seawater is usually between 32 ppt and 38 ppt.

Where there is a great deal of evaporation (the process by which a liquid changes into a gas due to an addition of heat

SALTS IN SEAWATER

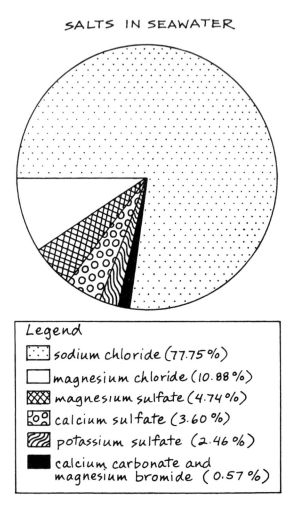

Legend

- [·····] sodium chloride (77.75%)
- [ ] magnesium chloride (10.88%)
- [XXXX] magnesium sulfate (4.74%)
- [o⁰] calcium sulfate (3.60%)
- [///] potassium sulfate (2.46%)
- [■] calcium carbonate and magnesium bromide (0.57%)

energy), the salinity of seawater increases. This occurs in areas of dry climate, such as the Mediterranean Sea, where the salinity is about 38 ppt. Where rivers enter the ocean, the salinity of seawater decreases to between 32 ppt and 35 ppt. This is because the salinity of the river water is very low, and it dilutes, or adds freshwater, to the seawater. Other areas of low salinity are cold icy bodies of water, such as the Arctic Ocean. Usually the melting ice and low evaporation keep the salinity of icy ocean waters lower than that of warmer ocean waters.

Water on land is not stationary, but continually moves toward the sea. As this water moves across the land, it picks up salts from the land and carries them to the sea. Some of these salts that are dumped into the sea settle to the bottom, and some dissolve in the seawater. Sea animals use calcium sulfate and calcium carbonate salts to make their shells and bones. The waters flowing into the seas from different places have dumped different salts into the ocean waters. The motion of ocean water thoroughly mix it. Thus samples of ocean water generally contain similar substances, whether at the poles or at the equator.

Although the ocean waters seem to have no place to go, and rivers continually pour water into them, the water level in the ocean does not continually rise. This is because water leaves the ocean by evaporation. The water lost through evaporation eventually returns to the ocean through the process of **condensation** (the process by which a gas changes into a liquid due to a removal of heat energy). This water returns to the earth as **precipitation** (liquid or solid particles of water that form in the atmosphere and then fall to the earth's surface), such as rain, hail, sleet, or snow. Precipitation falls into rivers and streams that flow over the land, bringing more water to the ocean. As long as the loss of water through evaporation equals the gain of water through precipitation, the water level in the ocean remains constant.

Let's Think It Through

1. The diagram on the next page shows two locations where water samples were taken. Which of the two samples, A or B, is more likely to have the lower salinity?

2. A 1,033 g sample of seawater has a salinity of 33 ppt. If all the water evaporated from the sample, how much salt would be left?

Answers

1. *Think!*

- Where rivers or streams enter the ocean, the salinity of seawater is lower.

- Location A is closer to where the river enters the ocean.

   Sample A should have the lower salinity of the two samples.

2. *Think!*

- Since the quantity unit of the seawater sample is the gram, the quantity unit of salt in the water will also be the gram. Thus, 33 ppt means that 33 g of salt are dissolved in 1,000 g of seawater.

    If all the water evaporates, 33 g of salt will be left.

Exercises

1. Samples of seawater were taken from three locations, A, B, and C. Which should have the highest salinity?

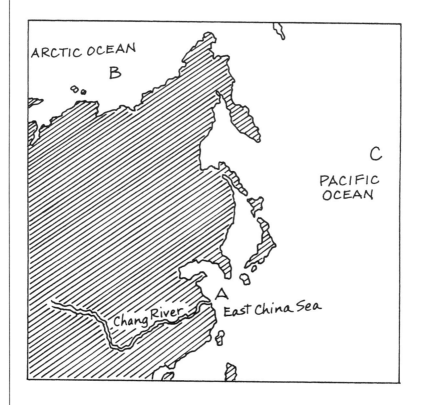

2. What is the salinity of a seawater sample that contains 36 pounds of salt per 1,000 pounds of seawater?

Activity: SUN DRIED

Purpose To use the sun to separate salt from salt water.

Materials cookie sheet
2 sheets of black construction paper
2 tablespoons (30 ml) table salt
1 cup (250 ml) tap water
spoon

Procedure

1. Cover the bottom of the cookie sheet with the black paper.

2. Add the salt to the water in the cup and stir. Most, but usually not all, of the salt will dissolve.

3. Pour the salty water over the paper. Try not to pour any undissolved salt onto the paper. Allow the undissolved salt to remain in the cup.

4. Place the cookie sheet in a sunny place where it will not be disturbed for several days. This can be by a window or outdoors if the weather is warm and dry.

5. Observe the paper daily until it is dry.

Results A thin layer of white crystals forms on the paper. A few small, white, cubic crystals form after several days.

Why? As the sun heats the salty water, the water evaporates and dry salt is left on the paper. This experiment is similar to a method used by some salt companies to produce salt by the evaporation of seawater. A **saltern** is a place where salt is produced by this method. A simple saltern can be made by digging a shallow pool near the sea and allowing seawater to flow in. The flow from the sea is then shut off to allow the sun to evaporate the water, leaving a deposit of salt crystals. This method of salt production is known as the **solar process,** and the product is called **solar salt.** Solar salt is still produced in large amounts in many countries, including the United States.

Solutions to Exercises

1. *Think!*

- Freshwater from the Chang River lowers the salinity of the East China Sea (location A).

- Melting ice and low evaporation lower the salinity of the icy water of the Arctic Ocean (location B).

  Location C, in the middle of the Pacific Ocean, should have the highest salinity of the three locations.

2. *Think!*

- Salinity is the measure of dissolved salts in seawater, in parts of salt per 1,000 parts of seawater (ppt).

- The sample contains 36 pounds of salt per 1,000 pounds of seawater.

  The salinity of the sample is 36 ppt.

15
Trashed

The Problems and Solutions of Ocean Pollution

What You Need to Know

Throughout history, people have dumped their garbage and other wastes into the ocean. In the past, there were fewer people and the ocean was so big that it could handle small amounts of **pollutants** (substances that destroy the purity of air, water, or land). When there were fewer people polluting the ocean with fewer, less harmful substances, the damage done was reversible, meaning that the waters would in time return to the way they were before being polluted.

Today, the amount of pollutants being dumped into the ocean is greater than ever before in the history of the earth. This is due to the increase in population. Along with the increase in population, there has been an increase in the amount of pollutants added to the ocean. The amount of garbage generated by each person varies from country to country, but in the United States each person generates about 5 pounds per day. Some of this trash ends up in the ocean, causing damage to the ocean that may not be reversible.

Garbage is a very visible form of ocean pollution. Ships frequently dump their trash into the sea, and some cities carry their trash out to sea and dump it. Some garbage, such as plastics, are not very **biodegradable** (able to break down into nonharmful substances by the action of living organisms, especially bacteria). Besides making the beaches dirty from trash that washes ashore, the contents of modern garbage can be dangerous to life in the ocean. For information about the effect of pollutants on marine life, see chapter 16, "Dumpster."

Most of the pollutants that enter the sea come from **raw sewage** (untreated liquid waste from drains, toilets, and sewers), poisonous metals, nuclear waste, chemical fertilizers, pesticides, oil, and other chemicals that wash into the ocean. Raw sewage can contain disease-causing bacteria. Poisonous metals such as mercury, lead, and tin come from factory and mine wastes. These metals are often taken in by fish and passed along to humans and other animals who eat them.

There are some laws that restrict cities and factories from dumping wastes into the ocean. But what can you do? Can a single person make a difference in the care of a body of water as big as the ocean? Yes! If everyone picked up some trash along the beach and disposed of it properly, or became involved in reusing and recycling everything possible—plastic containers, aluminum cans, glass, and paper—the ocean would be less polluted. Be on the alert to find ways to reduce the amount of garbage you generate each day, especially plastics.

Let's Think It Through

The pie chart shows the percentage of different items thrown overboard in a barrel of trash. Use the chart to answer the following questions:

1. Which type of material makes up the largest number of items thrown away?

2. Which type of material makes up the smallest number of items thrown away?

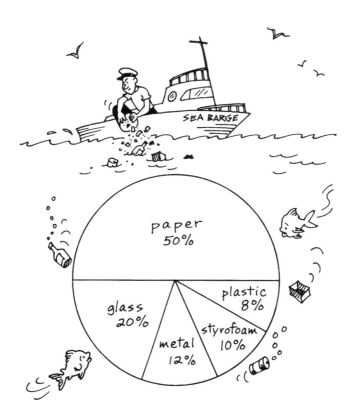

Answers

1. *Think!*

- The largest number of items are made of the material with the highest percentage.

  The largest number of items thrown away are made of paper.

2. *Think!*

- The smallest number of items are made of the material with the lowest percentage.

  The smallest number of items thrown away are made of plastic.

Exercises

The pie chart shows the percentage of items collected on a beach during a coastal cleanup campaign. Use the chart to answer the questions on the next page.

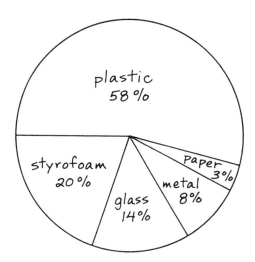

1. Which type of material makes up the largest number of items found?

2. Which type of material makes up the smallest number of items found?

Activity: RUNOFF

Purpose   To simulate how pollutants move from the land into the ocean.

Materials   long, shallow baking pan
cookie sheet
soil
trowel
red food coloring
tap water
2-quart (2-liter) pitcher

Procedure

1. Place the baking pan on the ground.

2. Place one end of the cookie sheet on the rim of one long edge of the baking pan, and use a mound of soil to raise the other end of the sheet about 4 inches (10 cm) above the rim of the pan.

3. Cover the surface of the cookie sheet with soil.

4. With permission, use the trowel to dig up 5 or 6 small clumps of grass, then set these on the soil-covered sheet.

NOTE: Grass clumps can be replaced in the ground when the experiment is completed.

5. Squeeze 5 to 6 drops of food coloring near the base of each clump of grass.

6. Half-fill the baking pan with water.

7. Fill the pitcher with water.

8. Hold the pitcher at the raised end of the cookie sheet and slowly pour the water across the soil at the raised end of the sheet.

9. Observe the color of the water washing into the pan of water.

Results   Water from the pitcher, along with bits of soil and red food coloring, wash into the pan.

Why?   Sources of pollution such as trash and oil spills are very visible and publicized, but one source that is very damaging to some coastal areas is polluted **runoff** (the part of precipitation that washes from the land into bodies of water). Runoff becomes polluted when rainwater runs across farmland, highways, city streets, lawns, mining areas, or any polluted place on the land. Fertilizers, pesticides, salt, oil, and all kinds of chemicals dissolve or float in the water and are carried to its final dumping place: the ocean.

In this experiment, the red food coloring represents fertilizer. The water from the pitcher (the rain) washes some of the soil and the fertilizer into the pan of water (the ocean). Fertilizers pollute because they provide too many **nutrients** (substances needed for the life and growth of living organisms), causing **algae** (plantlike organisms that contain chlorophyll and make their own food) and other plants to grow wildly. This fast productive growth is known as **algal bloom.** The algae and plants grow and eventually die. Bacteria feed on the dead algae and plants, and as they feed, the bacteria use up the oxygen in the water. This causes the water to contain less oxygen for the fish. Without enough oxygen, the fish and other animals in the water can suffocate.

Solutions to Exercises

1. *Think!*

- The largest number of items are made of the material with the highest percentage.

  The largest number of items found on the beach are made of plastic.

2. *Think!*

- The smallest number of items are made of the material with the lowest percentage.

  The smallest number of items found on the beach are made of paper.

16
Dumpster

How Pollutants Affect the Life of Animals in the Ocean

What You Need to Know

Since life began on earth, many **species** (a group of plants or animals that are alike in certain ways) of marine plants and animals have undergone **extinction** (dying out) due to natural processes. However, pollution causes or speeds up the extinction process. An **endangered species** is a species that is in immediate danger of becoming extinct. Many marine animals, such as the monk seal, blue whale, and loggerhead sea turtle, are presently endangered.

Humans have always treated the ocean as a big garbage dumpster. Some of the items thrown away can injure and even kill marine animals. Dolphins and other animals can become tangled in discarded fishing nets and drown. Plastic bags and balloons can be eaten by sea turtles who mistake them for jellyfish. The plastic blocks the turtle's digestive tract and it dies. Discarded plastic six-pack rings for holding canned drinks together can find their way around the bodies of animals. If the ring is caught around the neck or mouth, the animal can suffocate or die of starvation.

Oil in the ocean is another pollution problem that endangers marine animals. The oil makes the fur and feathers of some animals stick together, which affects the animals' movements. This mat-

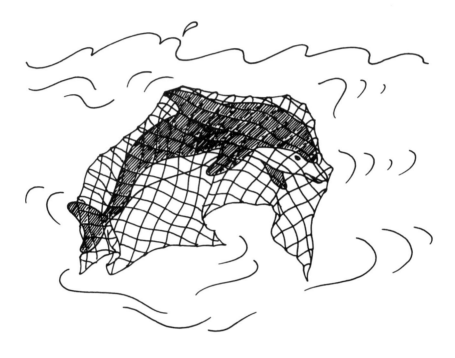

ted fur and feathers also pushes out the warm layer of air around the bodies of these animals, preventing them from staying warm. Oil can also suffocate and poison marine animals. Damage from oil does not occur only where the oil is released into the water. Oil floats on the water's surface, and currents can carry it long distances to harm marine life elsewhere.

Bioaccumulation is the process by which an animal gradually absorbs and stores a chemical in its body. Many animals in the ocean as well as some humans die from eating fish that have eaten a poisonous chemical. For example, a small fish takes in a tiny amount of a chemical pollutant released into the water from a factory. A larger fish feeds on many of the smaller fish, and it stores more of the pollutant in its body. The larger fish is eaten by a much larger fish, a dolphin, a seal, or maybe a human. If the degree of pollution is high enough, whatever eats the fish could become ill or die.

Pollutants are not the only thing endangering marine animals. **Overharvesting** (killing more of a species than can be replaced by reproduction) is a major problem. Some fish, sea turtles, whales, and other animals are killed by man in such numbers that they are not able to reproduce fast enough to keep pace.

Let's Think It Through

Study the direction of the South Equatorial Current between South America and Africa on the map on the next page. At which point, A or B, would an oil spill cause more damage to the coast-line of South America?

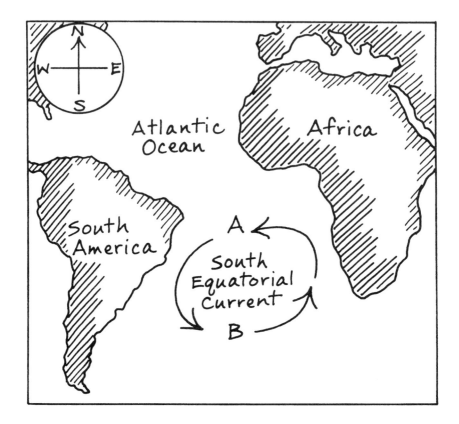

Answer

Think!

- Oil floats on the surface of water and is carried in the direction of the water's current.

- Toward which continent is the current moving from point A? South America.

- Toward which continent is the current moving from point B? Africa.

  An oil spill at point A would cause more damage to the coastline of South America.

Exercises

1. Study the diagram and the direction of the California Current along the West Coast of the United States. At which point would seals be safe from oil spilled at point B?

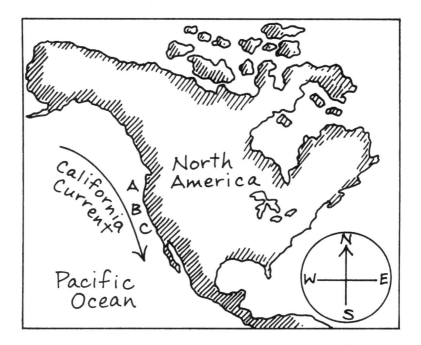

2. The skull and crossbones on the cans indicate that their contents are poisonous. Study the diagram on the next page to determine which fish has the most poison in its body as a result of the poisonous chemicals being dumped into the water.

Activity: COATED

Purpose   To demonstrate the effect that oil spills can have on birds.

Materials   2 small bowls
tap water
3 tablespoons (45 ml) oil

two 2- to 3-inch (5- to 7.5-cm) -long feathers (can be purchased at a crafts store)

NOTE: Do not pick up bird feathers from the ground outdoors; they can carry diseases.

Procedure

1. Fill the bowls three-fourths full with water.

2. Pour the oil into one of the bowls.

3. Gently lay one of the feathers on the surface of the water in the bowl without the oil.

4. Lift the feather from the bowl and blow on it.

5. Gently lay the second feather on the surface of the oil in the second bowl.

6. Lift the feather from the bowl and blow on it.

Results The feather taken from the water appears dry and is light enough to be moved by your breath. The feather taken from the oil appears wet and heavy. It moves little or not at all when you blow on it.

Why? Water does not stick to the feathers of birds very easily, but oil does. The oil-coated feather is very heavy, and the fibers of the feather stick together. This experiment demonstrates how oil from oil spills can mat the feathers of birds and make the birds too heavy to fly. This makes the birds easy prey to **predators** (animals that hunt and kill other animals for food).

Solutions to Exercises

1. *Think!*

- Oil floats on the surface of water and is carried along by currents.

- Toward which point is the current carrying the oil? Away from point A and toward points B and C.

Seals would be safe from the oil at point A.

2. *Think!*

- Fish A is small and takes in a tiny amount of poison directly from the water, which it stores in its body.

- Fish B is medium-size and feeds on two of the A fish. So fish B stores more poison in its body than does one of the A fish.

- Fish C is larger and feeds on two of the B fish. This means that fish C has more poison in its body than does fish B.

Fish C has the most poison in its body.

17
Changeable

How the Oceans Affect the Earth's Weather

What You Need to Know

Weather is the condition of the atmosphere in a specific place at a particular time. Ocean weather has its own special characteristics. The water from the ocean evaporates, making ocean winds more moist than those blowing off dry land. These wet winds generally make coastal areas wetter than inland areas. **Fog** (a cloud, the base of which is on or near the ground) and precipitation in the form of rain showers are not uncommon along the coast. The water carried to the land by winds eventually drains back into the ocean through runoff. This continuous movement of moisture from ocean to land and back again is called the **water cycle.**

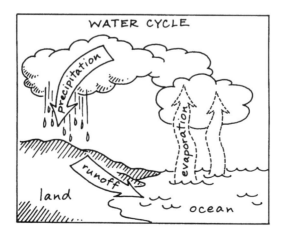

WATER CYCLE

precipitation

evaporation

runoff

land

ocean

Water heats and cools slowly. Once the ocean water has been heated by the sun, it holds the heat well. This means that at night, without the sun's heat, the temperature of the ocean water decreases very little. The overall effect of the ocean water's ability to retain heat well is that weather in coastal areas generally is less changeable than weather farther inland. Winters are warmer and summers are cooler.

Another characteristic of coastal areas is that they are usually very windy. The wind is due to the difference in how land and water absorb and lose heat from the sun. While the rate of gain and loss of heat is slow for water, the rate is fast for land. Thus, during the day, coastal land heats more quickly than the ocean water next to it. Since warm air is lighter than cool air, the warm air rises. The cooler air above the water rushes toward the land to take the place of the rising warm air. This movement of air from the ocean to the land is called a **sea breeze.** At night the land cools faster than the water. The warmer air above the water rises, and the cooler air above the land rushes toward the ocean. This movement of air from the land to the ocean is called a **land breeze.**

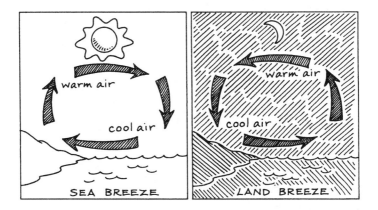

A **monsoon** (a seasonal wind caused by temperature differences between land and ocean) is a much larger example of sea and land breezes. Monsoon winds do not occur only on the coastline, but move inland. The largest monsoons occur in southern Asia. During the summer, the land heats and the air above the land rises. Cooler, moisture-filled air from the Indian Ocean moves in to replace the rising air. These winds bring clouds and heavy rains. During the winter, the monsoon blows in the opposite direction, from land to sea. The weather over the land is clear and dry.

A **cyclone** is a strong wind blowing in a circle. In the Northern Hemisphere, the winds of cyclones spin counterclockwise, and in the Southern Hemisphere, they spin clockwise. Cyclones that develop over the warm waters of the tropics are called **tropical cyclones.**

Tropical cyclones with winds of 74 miles per hour (118 kph) or more are called **hurricanes**. Hurricanes are called **typhoons** in the Western North Pacific Ocean and cyclones in the Indian Ocean. On the average, more than half of the world's tropical cyclones each year form in the Pacific Ocean, 24 percent in the Indian Ocean, and about 12 percent in the Atlantic Ocean.

The ocean weather at the equator is often calm and windless; this area of seemingly motionless air is called the **doldrums** (the region of little surface wind near the equator). Early sailors

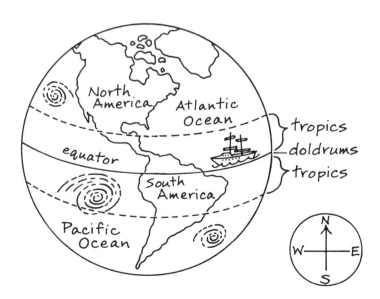

feared crossing into the doldrums because their ships depended on the wind to move them along. Without the wind, they could be stranded for long periods of time.

Let's Think It Through

Study the figures and determine which represents a sea breeze.

Answer

Think!

- Sea breezes blow during the day, and their direction is from the sea toward the land.

- In which figure are the flag and tree leaves blowing inland?

  Figure A represents a sea breeze.

Exercises

1. What are the names of the two tropical cyclones in the diagram?

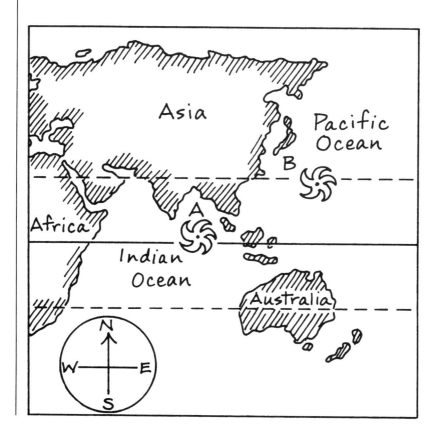

2. Which of the symbols represents a hurricane in the Atlantic Ocean above the equator?

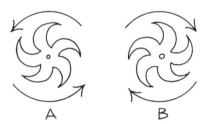

A   B

Activity: SPINNERS

Purpose   To determine the effect that warm water has on air movement above it.

Materials drawing compass
tissue paper
scissors
transparent tape
12-inch (30-cm) piece of thread
1 cup (250 ml) tap water
adult helper

Procedure

1. Use the compass to draw a 3-inch (7.5-cm) -diameter circle on the tissue paper.

2. Cut the circle into a spiral as shown by the dotted line.

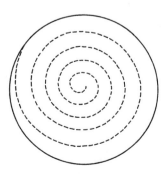

3. Tape one end of the piece of thread to the center of the paper spiral.

4. Ask an adult to heat the cup of water.

5. Holding the free end of the thread, position the bottom of the paper spiral about 2 inches (10 cm) above the cup of hot water.

Results The paper spiral twirls.

Why? Hurricanes, typhoons, and cyclones need moist air and heat to start them and keep them going. Both of these are abundant over tropical seas in late summer. The energy from the warm ocean water, like the hot water in the cup, heats the air above it. The air molecules move faster and farther apart as they absorb energy. The space between the molecules makes the air lighter, and the air rises upward. The rising warm air above the cup hits against the spiral and causes it to twirl. The twirling paper represents the twirling clouds of a hurricane, typhoon, or cyclone.

The warm, moist air above the ocean water rises and condenses to form clouds. The cooler surrounding air flows in to take the place of the rising warm air. Due to the rotation of the earth, the path of the cool air rushing in is curved. When the winds start to spin the clouds in a circle at a speed of less than 39 miles per hour (62 kph), the storm is considered a **tropical depression.** When the winds reach a speed of 39 miles per hour (62 kph), the storm is called a **tropical storm** and is officially named. When the winds reach a speed of 74 miles per hour (118 kph), it is classified as a hurricane, typhoon, or cyclone depending on its location.

Solutions to Exercises

1. *Think!*

- What is the name of a tropical cyclone that originates in the Indian Ocean?

  Tropical cyclone A is called a cyclone.

Think!

- What is the name of a tropical cyclone that originates in the western part of the North Pacific Ocean?

  Tropical cyclone B is called a typhoon.

2. *Think!*

- What direction do tropical cyclones spin above the equator? Counterclockwise.

- Which of the symbols shows a counterclockwise movement?

  Symbol A represents a hurricane in the Atlantic Ocean above the equator.

18
Floating Ice
The Formation and Characteristics of Icebergs

What You Need to Know

Glaciers are large bodies of land ice that flow slowly downhill. Glaciers form when the amount of snow falling in one place is greater than the amount of snow melting. As the snow piles up year after year, the increased weight creates pressure that **compresses** (squeezes together) the snow layers, trapping air in the ice. At the same time, water trickling in from thawing surface snow refreezes. The combination of pressure and refreezing turns the compressed snow to ice.

The underside of a glacier becomes soft because of the weight of the upper layers of ice. Bending around and pushing against obstacles creates enough friction to melt the bottom surface, which becomes slippery. In this way, glaciers are able to ooze very slowly downhill. The front, or lower, end of the glacier is called the **tongue,** "toe," or "snout." When the tongue of a glacier reaches the shoreline, the glacier is called a **tidal glacier.**

Because ice floats in water, the tongue of a tidal glacier that rests in water is pushed upward, and pieces of the tongue break off into the sea, forming **icebergs.** The process of iceberg formation is called **calving.** Calving can also occur if the glacier reaches the sea over a cliff. The tongue breaks off and falls into the sea. A third type of calving occurs if the portion of the glacier's tongue below the surface of the water is melted. The upper portion of the tongue is left without a support, and walls of ice break off into the sea. The calving process usually produces sounds like groans and rolling thunder as the ice cracks.

The size of icebergs can vary from small chunks, called "growlers" or "bergie bits," to king-size icebergs hundreds of feet tall and miles (kilometers) across. They also vary some in color. Some of the smaller icebergs melt in a few days or weeks, while the larger ones float around for years. Large or small, about four-fifths of an iceberg is under water.

The color of an iceberg depends on the amount of air trapped in the ice. The lower parts of an iceberg are more compressed and have very little trapped air. White light, such as sunlight, contains all the colors of the rainbow: red, orange, yellow, green, blue, indigo, and violet. These dense ice crystals absorb all the colors in sunlight except blue. This blue light is reflected in all directions, making the ice look blue. The upper layers and parts of the outer layers of some icebergs are less compressed and have more bubbles and cracks filled with air. This ice reflects all the colors in sunlight, which together produce white light. Thus, the light coming to your eyes from this ice appears white.

The main source of icebergs are the glaciers of Greenland and the continental shelf ice of Antarctica. The Antarctic icebergs are the largest. Icebergs are carried by currents toward the equator. Generally, Antarctic icebergs are not seen north of approximately 43°S. Thousands of icebergs are calved by the glaciers of Greenland. The currents around Greenland carry them southward, where they meet the Gulf Stream and the North Atlantic Drift. These currents spread them north-northeast across the Atlantic. Many melt during the journey, but some are seen all months of the year above 43°N. Few icebergs in the Arctic Ocean pass through the narrow Bering Strait connecting the Arctic Ocean with the Pacific Ocean. Thus, the Pacific is generally free of icebergs except below 43°S.

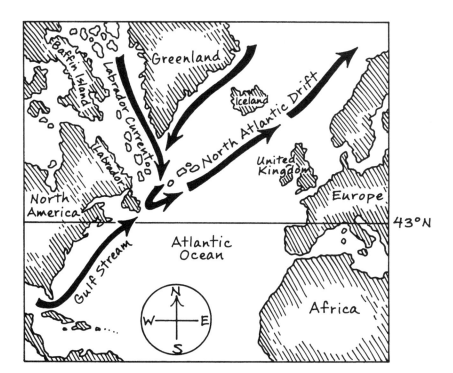

Let's Think It Through

1. Identify the figure that correctly shows how an iceberg floats in the ocean.

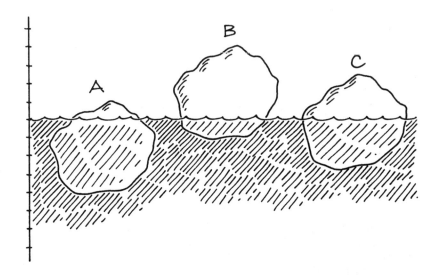

2. Identify the location on the map where an iceberg would more likely be found.

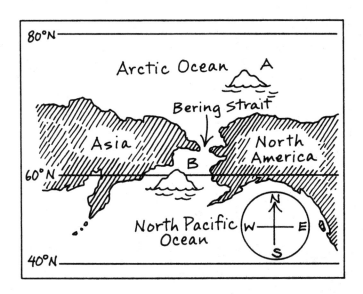

Answer

1. *Think!*

- About four-fifths of an iceberg is below the surface of the ocean.

  Iceberg A correctly shows how an iceberg floats.

2. *Think!*

- Icebergs are not usually found in the North Pacific because few pass through the Bering Strait.

  An iceberg would most likely be found at location A.

Exercises

1. If sunlight is striking compressed ice, which contains little or no trapped air, what color of light is being reflected in all directions by the ice?

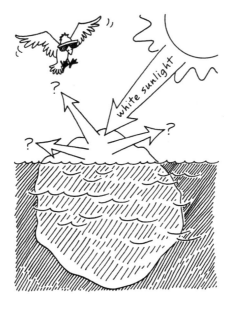

2. Identify the location on the map where an iceberg would more likely be found.

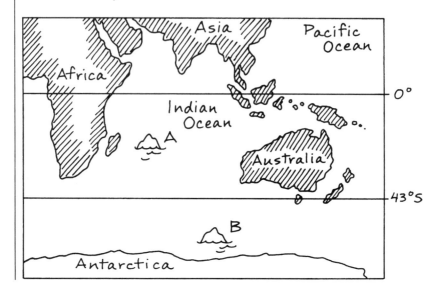

Activity: WATCH OUT BELOW!

Purpose   To demonstrate the position of an iceberg in water.

Materials   3-ounce (90-ml) paper cup
tap water
timer
wide-mouthed quart (liter) jar
2 teaspoons (10 ml) table salt
spoon

Procedure

NOTE: You must have access to a freezer.

1. Fill the cup with water.

2. Place the cup in the freezer for 2 hours or until the water in the cup is completely frozen.

3. Fill the jar three-fourths full with water.

4. Add the salt to the water in the jar and stir.

5. Remove the ice from the cup. To do this, wrap your hands around the cup for 5 to 6 seconds. The warmth from your hands melts some of the ice, making it easy to remove.

6. Tilt the jar and slowly slide the ice into the jar.

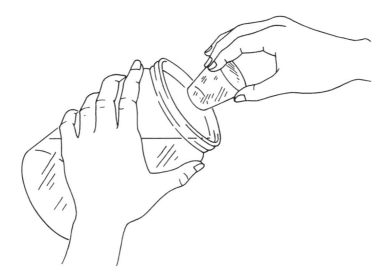

7. Observe the amount of ice above and below the surface of the water.

Results More ice is below the water's surface than above it.

Why? When water freezes, it expands. The density of ice is slightly less than the density of water. As a result, ice floats in water. Icebergs, like the ice in this experiment, float in seawater, which is salty. And like all floating ice, most of the ice is below the surface. Icebergs would float slightly lower in freshwater because the difference in density between ice and freshwater is less than that between ice and seawater.

Solutions to Exercises

1. *Think!*

- Compressed ice, with little or no trapped air, absorbs all the colors of sunlight except blue.

  The light reflected off the ice is blue.

2. *Think!*

- Antarctic icebergs are generally found below 43°S.

  An iceberg would more likely be found at location B.

19
Layered

Types of Ocean Life and Their Environment

What You Need to Know

Marine organisms are classified according to their habits and the part of the ocean where they live. **Plankton** is a term for small, often microscopic organisms that drift with the current or tide at or near the ocean's surface. Most cannot move by themselves. Plantlike plankton capable of producing food by **photosynthesis** (the food-making reaction in plants, using carbon dioxide, water, and sunlight), such as algae, are called **phytoplankton.** The animal form of plankton, such as **krill** (small shrimplike animals), are called **zooplankton. Nekton** are all organisms in the ocean that can swim, from the smallest fish to

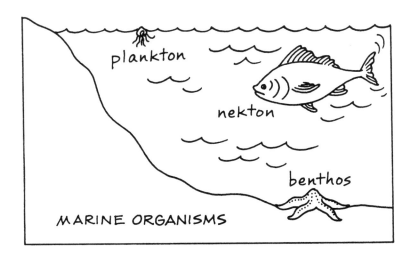

plankton

nekton

benthos

MARINE ORGANISMS

the largest whale. **Benthos** are all creatures that live on the ocean floor, such as starfish, worms, clams, and snails.

The ocean can be divided into three zones according to the presence of sunlight: the sunlight zone, the twilight zone, and the midnight zone. The zones also differ in temperature, amount of water pressure, and available nutrients. These differences affect the type of life that can survive in each zone.

The top layer, called the **sunlight zone,** has the most light. On the average, most of the sunlight is absorbed by the water between the surface and a depth of 300 feet (90 m), but the lower boundary of the zone can extend to a depth of 600 feet (180 m) or more. This is the smallest zone, but contains more than 90 percent of marine life. Since plants require sunlight to live, this is the area where plants are most productive.

The **twilight zone** starts from the bottom of the sunlight zone and extends down to about 3,000 feet (900 m) below the surface. As the depth increases, the water gets darker, its temperature decreases, and its pressure increases. There is very little light entering this zone, and the light is mostly blue and violet. Green plants are not able to grow in this zone. There is less food in this area, so there is less animal life. Many animals here feed off of falling remains of dead organisms from the sunlight zone. Some swim to the sunlight zone at night to feed off the nutrients there. Some animals in this zone glow in the dark, using special organs that give off light. The process by which living organisms produce light is called **bioluminescence.**

The **midnight zone** extends from the bottom of the twilight zone to the ocean floor. The only light in this zone is produced by bioluminescence. The greatest source of nutrients is the remains of marine life from the ocean's upper zones. There are fewer life-forms in this area because of the darkness, low temperatures, high water pressure, and scarce food supplies. The animals living here generally grow very slowly and live for a longer period of time because the speed of the body's chemical and physical activities is slow.

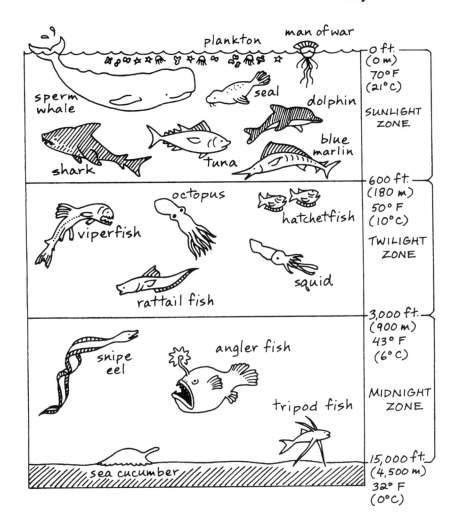

Let's Think It Through

Sunlight is made up of many colors, and each color can travel a certain distance in seawater. The graph on the next page shows the depth where most of each color of light is absorbed. Use the graph to answer the following questions:

1. Which color of light reaches the greatest depth?

2. Which color(s) reach a depth of 80 feet (24 m)?

3. To what depth are all the colors present?

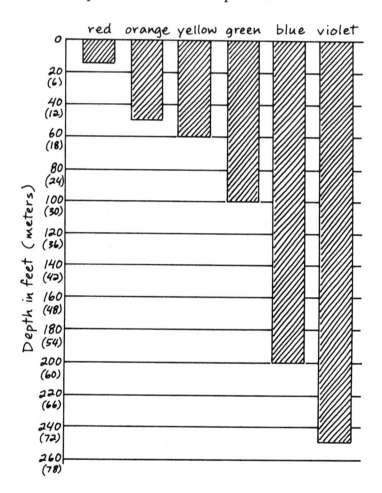

Answers

1. *Think!*

- The longest bar indicates the greatest depth.
- Which color has the longest bar?

  Violet light reaches the greatest depth.

2. *Think!*

• Which color(s) shown by the bars reach or pass the 80-foot (24-m) mark?

Green, blue, and violet light reach a depth of 80 feet (24 m).

3. *Think!*

• The shortest bar is the depth where all the colors appear.

• What is the depth of the shortest bar?

All the colors are present to a depth of about 15 feet (4.5 m).

Exercises

Water pressure increases with depth. Use the graph to answer the questions on the next page.

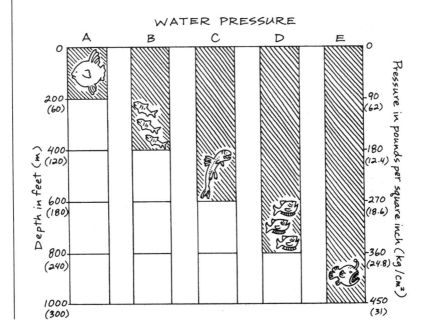

1. Which fish has the least pressure on its body?

2. How many fish have 270 pounds per square inch (18.6 kg/cm²) or more pressure on their bodies?

Activity: TOO DARK

Purpose To demonstrate why most marine plants are found in the ocean's sunlight zone.

Materials small cooking pot
plot of grass

Procedure

1. With adult approval, place the pot upside down on the grass.

2. At the end of 10 days, lift the pot and compare the color of the grass covered by the pot with the grass around the outside of the pot.

Results   The grass that was covered by the pot is pale yellow, while the grass around the outside of the pot is green.

Why?   Marine plants, like all plants, need sunlight to undergo photosynthesis, the energy-making reaction that provides them with food. **Chlorophyll,** a green pigment found in plants, is necessary for photosynthesis. Without sunlight, the chlorophyll molecules do not develop, causing the plant to look pale. In time, all plants, including grass, will die without sunlight.

Green plants grow abundantly at the top of the sunlight zone—the ocean's surface—and decrease in number with depth. At the bottom of the sunlight zone—600 feet (180 m)—there are few to no green plants. This is because most of the sunlight is absorbed by the water before it reaches this depth.

Solutions to Exercises

1. *Think!*

- The least pressure is at the least depth.
- The shortest bar indicates the least depth.
- Which fish is at the shortest bar?

  Fish A has the least pressure on its body.

2. *Think!*

- How many bars reach or pass the 270-pound (18.6-kg) mark?

  Three fish, C, D, and E, have 270 pounds per square inch (18.6 kg/cm^2) or more pressure on their bodies.

20
Sea Café

Relationships between Marine Food Producers and Food Consumers

What You Need to Know

Penguins eat small fish; leopard seals eat penguins; killer whales eat leopard seals. These organisms are linked together because each one is food for the next. This type of connection is called a **food chain.**

Marine plants and animals may be food for different kinds of animals, and most animals eat more than one kind of food. Thus, many animals belong to several different food chains, that are interlinked to form a **food web.** While definite food webs can be identified within specific ocean zones, animals from one food web will feed off plants and animals from another. This creates one massive interlinked food web composed of all life in the ocean.

The source of energy in most marine food chains is the sun. Marine plants, like land plants, use the sun's energy to produce their own food by photosynthesis. Thus, plants are called **producers** because they produce food from nonliving matter. The most important producers in the ocean are phytoplankton.

Consumers are organisms that cannot produce their own food and must eat other organisms. Organisms that feed on phytoplankton, such as zooplankton, clams, and corals, are at the

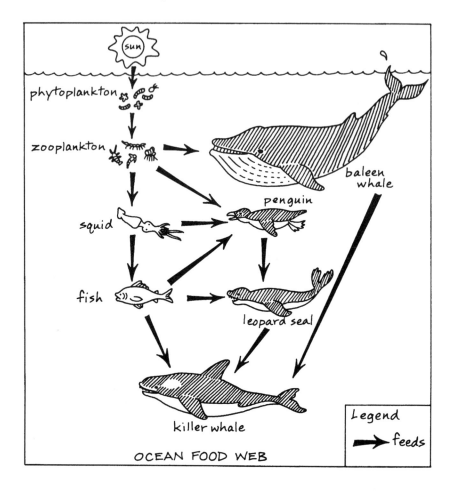

OCEAN FOOD WEB

start of the marine food chain. The chain continues, first with animals, such as squid, penguins, and even baleen whales, that eat the zooplankton, and then with the other large animals, such as leopard seals, fish, and killer whales, that eat the animals that dine on zooplankton. In other words, the ocean is like an unusual café where the customer eats its meal, but may become the meal for the next customer on the scene.

Let's Think It Through

Considering only the organisms in the Ocean Food Chain diagram on the next page, what would happen to the other organisms in the food chain if the penguin became ill and died? Choose the best answer from the following:

a. There would be an increase in small fish and a decrease in zooplankton.

b. All the organisms would die.

OCEAN FOOD CHAIN

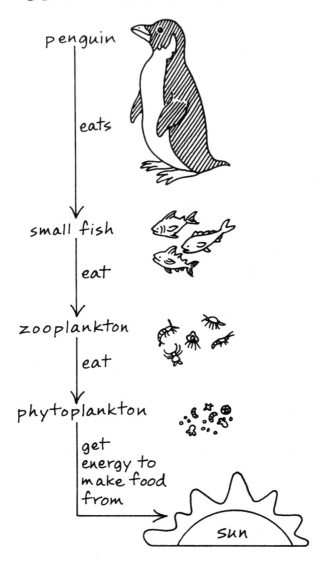

penguin

eats

small fish

eat

zooplankton

eat

phytoplankton

get
energy to
make food
from

sun

Answer

Think!

- Without the penguins to kill them, who would be at the top of the food chain? The small fish.

- If the number of small fish increased, would they eat more or fewer zooplankton? They would eat more zooplankton.

The best answer is a. There would be an increase in small fish and a decrease in zooplankton.

Exercises

A special ocean-floor food chain exists in the deep sea around an area of hot, mineral-rich water escaping through cracks in the earth's crust. Unlike other deep-sea bottom dwellers, these organisms such as 8-foot (2.4-m) -long tube worms, are large in size and number, grow quickly, and do not depend on falling dead material from surface water for food. Use the Marine "Hot Spot" Food Chain chart to answer the questions on the next page.

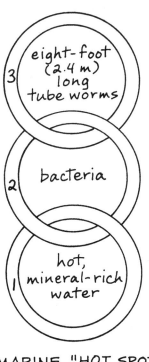

MARINE "HOT SPOT"
FOOD CHAIN

1. This food chain does not depend on the sun for its energy source. What is its source of energy?

2. Plants use sunlight to make food. What do the bacteria use to make food?

Activity: BALANCED

Purpose   To demonstrate the balance between consumers and producers.

Materials masking tape
pencil with flat sides
two 5-ounce (150-ml) or similar-size paper cups
ruler
walnut-size piece of modeling clay
box of small paper clips

Procedure

1. Tape the pencil to a table so that the pencil rests on one of its flat sides and the pencil point faces you.

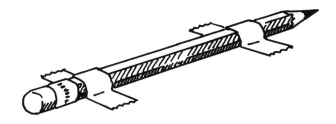

2. Tape 1 cup to each end of the ruler as shown in the illustration.

3. Position the center of the ruler on the pencil.

4. Shape a small fish from the clay.

5. Place the clay fish in one of the cups.

6. Add paper clips to the other cup until the cups balance (the ends of the ruler will no longer touch the tabletop).

paper clip

tiny clay fish

Results   When enough paper clips were added, the cups balanced.

Why?   The paper clips represent producers, and the clay fish represent consumers. Consumers feed off producers. At first, as you began to add paper clips, the two cups were not balanced. This represents a situation where there are not enough producers in an area to feed the consumers. In this situation, the consumers will die if they are not able to move to a location with enough food. When the cups balance, the model represents a situation where the number of food producers in an area is enough to feed the consumers present.

Solutions to Exercises

1. *Think!*

- The first link in the chain represents the energy source.
- What makes up the chain's first link?

  Hot, mineral-rich water is the energy source of the marine "hot spot" food chain.

2. *Think!*

- What is below bacteria in the food chain?

  Bacteria use hot, mineral-rich water to make food.

21
Bottom Dwellers
Plant and Animal Life in the Different Ocean Floor Zones

What You Need to Know

Ocean **environments** (the surroundings of living things) can be divided into two main areas: the open ocean and the ocean floor. The types of plants and animals found in these two environments usually differ in many ways. Information about the open ocean can be found in chapter 19, "Layered."

The ocean floor can be divided into three major zones: the beach area, where the tides rise and fall, called the **shore zone;** the floor from the low-tide line to the edge of the continental shelf, called the **neritic zone;** and the floor beneath the waters in the open ocean, called the **deep-sea zone.** Each zone has very different kinds and numbers of organisms.

The organisms of the shore zone have to endure daily changes, since the shore is wet part of the day and dry part of the day as the waters rise and fall with the tides. Many plants and animals cling to rocks to remain stationary as the waters move. Some, such as clams and periwinkles, have hard shells that protect them when the tide is out, and others, such as crabs and lugworms, bury themselves in wet sand.

The neritic zone starts at the low-tide line and extends into the ocean. From the top of the zone to about 300 feet (90 m), it is often warm and has plenty of light, so plants such as sea grasses, kelp, and other seaweeds are found here. This part of the ocean floor is brimming with various forms of animal life that crawl on, stick to, tunnel through, and swim near the bottom. The floor is rich with nutrients from decaying plant and animal life. As the waters are stirred by winds, these nutrients are lifted to the surface where animals living near the surface feed.

The deep-sea zone is the deepest part of the ocean floor. The remains of decayed organisms falling to the bottom over thousands of years have produced a thick layer of sediments called ooze deposits at the bottom of the ocean. There are no plants in this zone, because sunlight cannot reach the bottom. The deep-sea zone has the least number of animals compared to the other ocean floor zones. Some animals, such as the sea cucumber, crawl or tunnel into the ooze; others, such as the tripod fish, have spines, long legs, or hairs so they can move in the ooze without sinking. However, few animals live on the floor in this area. In fact, most of the floor of the deep-sea zone is deserted.

Let's Think It Through

Identify the figure that correctly represents plant growth on the ocean floor.

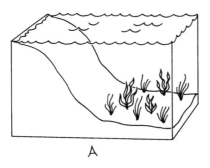

A

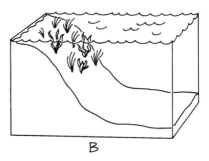

B

Answer

Think!

- Light is required for plant growth.

- Light reaches the ocean floor under water to a depth of about 300 feet (90 m).

- Which diagram shows plant growth in shallow water, but not in deep water?

Figure B represents plant growth on the ocean floor.

Exercises

1. Does the diagram represent the order of the ocean floor zones?

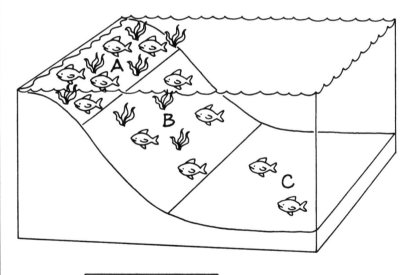

2. Identify the fish that is best structured to move along the bottom of the deep-sea zone without sinking into the ooze.

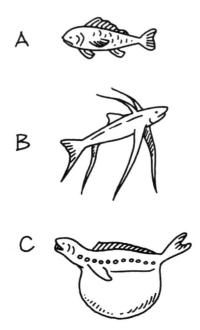

A

B

C

Activity: **MIGRATING EYE**

Purpose   To show how an adult flatfish develops to live on the ocean floor.

Materials   lemon-size piece of modeling clay
2 pinto beans
sheet of typing paper

Procedure

1. Mold the clay into the shape of a fish with a slightly rounded body.

2. Place a bean on each side of the fish's head.

3. Place the paper on a table and stand the fish, belly side down, on the paper.

4. Observe the shape of the body and the location of the beans.

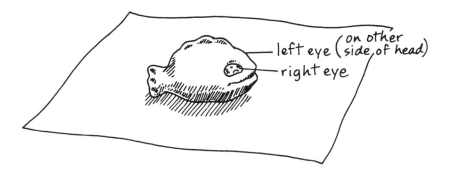

5. Move the left-eye bean to the top of the fish's head.

6. Lean the fish onto its left side, and slightly flatten its body ‚and head.

7. Again observe the location of the beans and the shape of the fish's body.

8. Move the left-eye bean again, nearer the right-eye bean.

9. Press the fish's body and head flat as shown in the diagram.

10. Observe the final location of the beans and the shape of the fish's body.

Results   The bean on the left side of the fish's head is moved around the head in stages so that both beans lie on one side—the right side—of the head. The fish's body is changed from a round form to a flat form.

Why?   The beans represent the eyes of a flatfish, such as a flounder. All young flatfish have the general shape of other fish: a rounded body with eyes on either side of their head. The clay model in this experiment does not change in size, but in nature the young flatfish starts to grow larger and its body starts changing. One eye slowly starts to move over the top of the head. At this point, the fish moves to the ocean floor and lies on its blind side. In a short time, the body is greatly flattened from side to side and the two eyes are close together on the upper, sighted side of the head. About three-fourths of flatfish lie on their left side.

Flatfish are found in all parts of the world. They swim on or near the ocean bottom. Their two eyes work independently of each other, so they can see in all directions. Their upper side is similar in color to the ocean floor where they lie, and some flatfish are able to change coloration, like the lizard called a chameleon, to better camouflage themselves.

Solutions to Exercises

1. *Think!*

- The beach area called the shore zone has plants and animals.

- The second zone, called the neritic zone, has the most plants and animals.

- The third zone has no plants and few animals.

  The diagram does not represent the order of the ocean floor zones; the order should be B, A, C.

2. *Think!*

- To prevent them from sinking, animals living in the ooze deposits need some type of support, such as stalks.

  Fish B, called a tripod fish, has long stalklike fins that prevent it from sinking into the ooze in the deep-sea zone.

22
Movers

Learning How Marine Life Moves

What You Need to Know

Marine animals come in all shapes and sizes and move in many different ways. Most marine animals move around to find food, or to find a mate, or to escape from a predator. Some ocean creatures such as swordfish, rapidly move from one place to the other in search of food. They can race through the water chasing food at more than 68 miles per hour (109 kph). Others, such as garden eels, can move, but usually stay in one place. Garden eels live, tails down, in holes in the sand. They stick their heads out of the sand to catch food that drifts by.

GARDEN EELS

SWORDFISH

Some marine animals can even perform fantastic feats when they move, such as the 50-foot (15.5-m) humpback whale, which can burst into the air and do a backward somersault. Springing of a whale from the water is called **breaching.** Some whales can also move into a vertical position with their heads out of the water. This position is known as **spy-hopping.**

Some tiny marine animals do not move on their own. Instead, they are carried from place to place by ocean currents. The balloon-shaped body of the Portuguese man-o'-war allows it to float on the surface and drift with the wind. Some of the torpedo-shaped squid can propel themselves by squirting water out of nozzles on their bodies. The squid can swim so fast that it can shoot out of the water and glide through the air for long distances. The spiny-armed starfish have tube feet with suckers at the end. When they extend their feet, the suckers stick to an object ahead of the animal. Then, the foot is shortened to pull the starfish along.

Most fish have several **fins** (the usually flat body parts on a fish that are used for movement and balance) that all work together to move the fish through the water. A fish swims by moving its tail, the caudal fin, from side to side. The paired fins on either side of the fish's body, the pectoral and pelvic fins, are used to steer and balance the fish. For swimming quickly, these fins are usually held flat against the fish's body. By extending all four of these fins at the same time, the fish uses the fins as a brake, allowing the fish to stop quickly. The single dorsal and anal fins, on the top

FINS OF A FISH

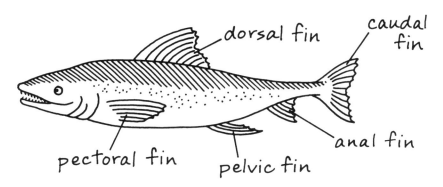

and bottom of the fish, respectively, prevent the fish from rocking from side to side.

Most fish have a **swim bladder** (an air-filled sac inside a fish's body), which allows the fish to float. Air can enter this bladder either through the fish's mouth or from the bloodstream. As the bladder expands with air, the fish rises in the water. The fish sinks in the water as the bladder deflates. Fish that do not have a swim bladder, such as sharks, must swim continuously to keep from sinking.

Let's Think It Through

Study the position of the fins of each fish in the figures. Which position of the fins allows the fish to swim faster?

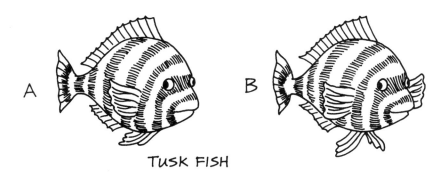

TUSK FISH

Answer

Think!

- The closer the fins are to the body, the faster the fish can swim.
- Extending the fins from the body helps the fish to stop.
- Which fish has its fins closer to its body?

  The position of the fins in figure A allows the fish to swim faster.

Exercises

1. Which figure shows a whale that is spy-hopping?

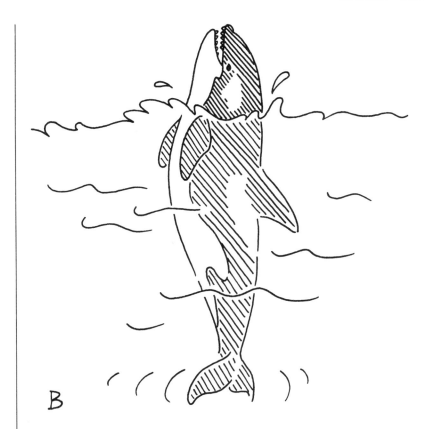

B

2. Which fish is swimming at a greater depth?

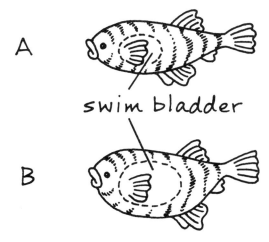

A

swim bladder

B

Activity: FLOATERS

Purpose   To determine how a swim bladder allows a fish to move up and down in the water.

Materials   quart (liter) wide-mouthed jar
tap water
2 glass marbles
two 7-inch (17.5-cm) round balloons

Procedure

1. Fill the jar three-fourths full with water.

2. Place 1 marble inside each balloon.

3. In one of the balloons, tie a knot as close to the marble as possible.

4. Drop the balloon in the jar of water.

5. Slightly inflate the second balloon with air, and tie a knot as close to the mouth of the balloon as possible.

6. Drop this balloon in the jar of water.

Results The inflated balloon floats on the surface of the water, but the deflated balloon sinks to the bottom of the jar.

Why? When an object is in water, the water molecules push upward on the object. If the object doesn't weigh too much, the water molecules under the object can lift it to the surface and hold it there. Thus, the object floats. The object sinks if its weight is more than the water molecules can lift. The amount of air in the balloon has little weight. So the weight of the balloons with or without air is about the same. However, the air in the balloon makes the balloon larger, and since it takes up more space in the water, there are more water molecules pushing up on the balloon. Thus, the balloon floats. The swim bladder in a fish behaves like the balloon. As the amount of air inside the fish's bladder increases, the fish enlarges and is lifted toward the water's surface.

Solutions to Exercises

1. *Think!*

• Which whale is in a vertical position with its head out of the water?

The killer whale in figure B is spy-hopping.

2. *Think!*

• The swim bladder inflates to allow the fish to float.

• The smaller or more deflated the swim bladder, the deeper the fish can swim.

• Which fish has the smaller swim bladder?

Fish A is swimming at a greater depth.

23
Ocean Giants
Learning about Whales

What You Need to Know

Scientists put organisms that have certain things in common, such as what they look like and where they live, into big groups. These groups are called **orders**. Whales, dolphins, and porpoises belong to the order Cetacea. Orders can be separated into smaller groups, called **families**. The two cetacean families are toothed whales and baleen whales. Toothed whales, such as killer whales, dolphins, and porpoises, have teeth and hunt for food, such as fish and squid. Baleen whales, such as the blue whale and humpback whale, have sheets of horny material, called **baleens**, that hang down from their upper jaws instead of teeth. Baleens work like large strainers. Water passes through, but tiny fish and shrimp get caught. The whale eats the food trapped in the baleen.

TOOTHED WHALE

BALEEN WHALE

Baleen whales are the largest animals living in the ocean or on earth. An adult blue whale may be over 100 feet (30 m) long and weigh over 400,000 pounds (181,800 kg). But all baleen whales are not this large, and the toothed whales range in size from the 4-to-6-foot (1.2-to-1.8 m) -long porpoise, weighing from 110 to 165 pounds (50 to 74 kg), to the 60-foot (18-m) sperm whale, weighing about 91,000 pounds (41,400 kg).

Although whales live in water and look much like fish, they are really mammals. **Mammals** are **warm-blooded** (having a body temperature that does not change with the surroundings) animals with a backbone. A thick layer of **blubber** (threadlike tissue filled with oil) under the whale's skin helps to keep the animal warm. Female mammals have glands that produce milk for feeding their young and give birth to live young instead of laying eggs as fish do. Like all mammals, whales have lungs to breathe in oxygen from the air, while fish have **gills** to get oxygen from the water. Whales, being air breathers, must rise to the surface to breathe. They normally breathe about once every 5 minutes, but can remain under water for much longer periods of time.

Whales are found in all oceans. Their bodies are covered with skin that is almost completely hairless. The tail makes up one-third of the whale's body. At the end of the tail is a fin called a **fluke.** Some whales, such as the killer whale, have two flukes. The fluke runs sideways, instead of up and down like a fish's tail. Whales swim by beating their tails up and down. These straight up-and-down movements of its tail and fluke allow the whale to move speedily through the water. Some whales can swim as fast as 45 miles per hour (72 kph). The strength of the tail allows the whale to dive very deep in the water and then push itself up to the surface of the ocean to breathe.

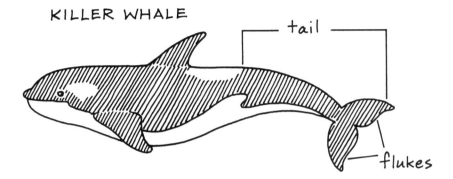

KILLER WHALE
tail
flukes

Like other mammals, whales breathe through an opening in the head called a **nostril.** Most mammals have two nostrils, but the whale has only one nostril, on top of its head, called the **blowhole.** The whale inhales slowly, but exhales very rapidly and with great force. It seems as though a spout of water is blown into the air each time the whale exhales. Actually, the warm moist breath from its body contains **water vapor** (water in the gas state), which condenses when it meets the cooler air outside the whale's body. A cloud usually called "steam" is formed. This cloud is like that seen escaping from a heated teapot or your "steamy" breath on a cold winter day.

The whale's brain is larger than that of any other animal. Scientists believe that the whale is the most intelligent animal in the ocean. The whale's eyes, though small, give it good vision above and below water, but its sense of smell is poor or absent. Its sense of hearing is very sharp, and the whale can produce sounds. The bottle-nosed dolphin whistles, barks, and makes snapping sounds. Sounds from other whales may be high-pitched squeals, ticks, clucks, chirps, and even mewing sounds. Whales communicate with these sounds, but they also use them to locate objects. Using sound to locate objects is called **echo sounding.** By bouncing sounds off an object and listening for the echoes, the whale can determine the distance of the object and move through pitch-black waters without hitting the object.

Let's Think It Through

Use the bar graph to answer the following questions:

1. Which whale can stay under water the longest?

2. How long can the sperm whale stay under water?

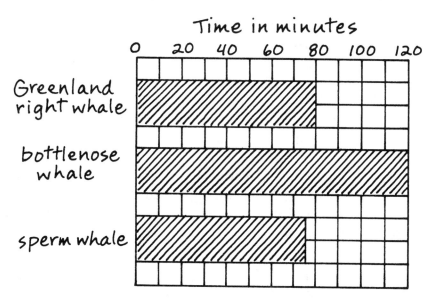

Answers

1. *Think!*

- Which whale is shown next to the longest bar?

   The bottlenose whale can stay under water the longest.

2. *Think!*

- The numbering on the horizontal scale indicates that each square equals 10 minutes. One-half of a square equals 5 minutes.

- The sperm whale's time is shown by $7\frac{1}{2}$ squares.

- A time of $7\frac{1}{2}$ squares equals:

$(7 \times 10) + 5 = ?$

The sperm whale can stay under water for 75 minutes.

Exercises

1. Use the bar graph to answer the following questions. Determine all speeds in both miles per hour (mph) and kilometers per hour (kph).

a. Which is the fastest whale?

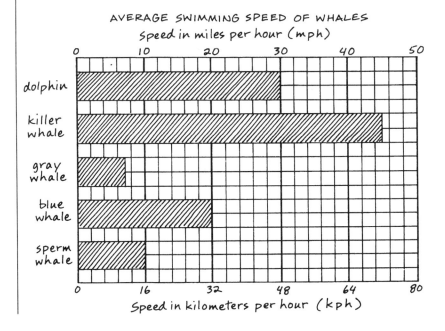

AVERAGE SWIMMING SPEED OF WHALES
Speed in miles per hour (mph)

b. If man can swim at a speed of 3 mph (4.8 kph), how many whales are faster than man?

2. Which figure(s) are similar to what appears to be a spout of water spraying out of a whale's blowhole?

Activity: BLUBBER

Purpose   To demonstrate that blubber under a whale's skin keeps the animal warm.

Materials two 7-ounce (210-ml) paper cups
cotton balls
2 bulb-type thermometers
¾ cup (188 ml) cooking oil
timer

Procedure

1. Cover the inside bottom of one of the cups with a layer of cotton balls.

2. Stand one of the thermometers on the layer of cotton balls.

cotton balls

3. Fill the cup with cotton balls.

4. Slowly pour the oil into the cotton-filled cup.

5. Stand the second thermometer in the second, empty cup.

   NOTE: Lay the cup on its side if the weight of the thermometer tends to topple the cup over.

6. Read and record the temperature shown on each thermometer. Then, place the cups with their thermometers in the freezer and shut the door.

oil-soaked cotton balls

7. Read and record the temperature shown on each thermometer at the end of 30 minutes.

Results   The reading on the thermometer placed in the oil-soaked cotton changed very little, but the temperature inside the empty cup decreased greatly.

Why?   Heat energy moves from a warmer place to a cooler place. When heat energy moves away from an object, that object becomes cooler and its temperature drops. **Insulators** are materials that slow down the transfer of heat energy. Under the paper-thin, hairless skin of a whale lies a thick layer of blubber. The oil-soaked cotton threads, like the blubber layer in whales, act as an insulator by limiting the heat flow away from them, just as blubber helps keep the whale's body heat from escaping into the cooler water outside its body. The heat inside the oily cotton, like that in a whale's body, is lost, but because of the insulating blubber, the loss is slower. In spite of the insulating blubber layer, most whales at rest lose more heat than they produce and therefore swim to keep warm.

Solutions to Exercises

1a. *Think!*

- Which whale has the longer bar?

The killer whale is the fastest whale.

b. *Think!*

- The numbering on the horizontal scales indicates that each square equals 2 mph (3.2 kph). One-half of a square equals 1 mph (1.6 kph).
- A speed of 3 mph (4.8 kph) is shown by 1½ squares.
- How many bars are longer than 1½ squares?

All the whales—dolphin, killer, gray, blue, and sperm— can swim faster than man.

2. *Think!*

- Which figure(s) show a "steam" cloud being produced when warm moist air hits cooler air?

Figures B and C are similar to what appears to be a spout of water spraying out of a whale's blowhole.

24
Lookers

Learning How Some Ocean Creatures See

What You Need to Know

The simplest organs of sight are called **eyespots.** Eyespots are not eyes at all, but light-sensitive areas that detect differences between light and dark. Many single-celled marine organisms need sunlight to survive, but can be damaged if the light is too strong. (A **cell** is the smallest building block of all living things.) These organisms have eyespots to direct them toward moderate light, but away from strong harsh rays that could injure them. Larger marine organisms, such as the starfish and scallop, also have eyespots. The eyespot of a starfish is located at the tip of each arm. A scallop may have several hundred eyespots all around the edges of its shell. Each eyespot acts as a simple eye that cannot **focus** (sharpen the image of an object).

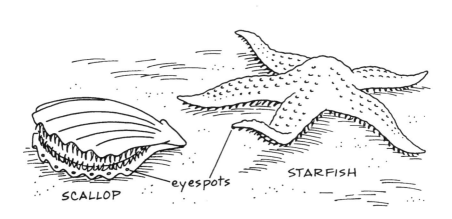

eyespots

STARFISH

SCALLOP

Although the images from these eyespots are not clear, the scallop can catch sight of approaching danger, such as a hungry starfish, and escape.

Many marine creatures are able to see in all directions at once because of the location of their eyes. Most fish have eyes positioned on opposite sides of their heads, which permits them to see all around them. The flounder, unlike most other fish, has both eyes on the same side of its head. This works well for a bottom dweller like the flounder, since it lies on one side on the bottom of the ocean. If the flounder's eyes were on either side of its body, one eye would always be pressed into the ocean bottom. Fish have a wide field of vision, but most have **monocular vision** (separate images viewed by each eye). Because two separate images are seen by the two eyes, it is difficult for fish to determine distances. Other creatures, such as the fiddler crab, have eyes on movable stalks. The crab buries itself in sand to hide from its enemies. It can raise its eyes like the periscopes on a submarine to see if it is safe to come out of hiding. The images the crab sees are not as clear as the ones you see, but its eyes are very sensitive to motion.

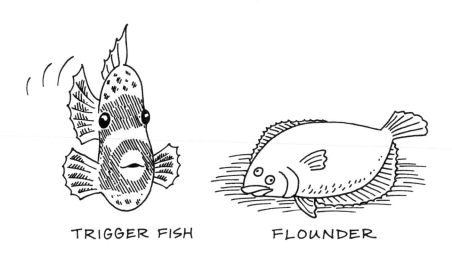

TRIGGER FISH   FLOUNDER

FIDDLER CRAB

Your eyelids are folds of skin that cover or uncover your eyeballs. When you blink, the lids close to protect your eyes and to carry cleansing tears to wash the eyes. Most fish do not have eyelids. Instead, the eyes are protected by a tough, glassy coating. The open eyes are constantly washed by the water the fish swims in. The puffer fish has another way of protecting its eyes. When alarmed, the puffer blows itself up with water. Muscles around its eyes contract, forming what appears to be lidlike pouches. These pouches partially cover the eyes, leaving only a tiny slit.

Marine organisms living far below the ocean's surface have very little light with which to see. At depths where there is less and less light, organisms have larger and larger eyes. In the areas of lowest light, the eyes of some fish are tubular. Each tube is lined with light-sensitive tissue, and a ball-shaped **lens** (the part of the eye that focuses light rays) rests at the top of the tube. The light-sensitive tissue helps the fish see in its dimly lighted surroundings, but overall, the things seen are out of focus. As one descends from depths with the least amount of light into the pitch-black areas of the ocean, the eyes of the fish become smaller and smaller. Many deep-sea fish have very undeveloped eyes or no eyes at all.

A whale has good vision both below and above water. It also has relatively good vision at depths where light levels are very low. Another marine creature with good eyesight is the octopus. This creature has eye parts similar to those of your own eye.

Let's Think It Through

The diagram shows two groups of single-celled marine organisms. Each organism has an eyespot. If the area of the ocean closest to the sun in the diagram provides the strongest sunlight, which is the correct location for the organisms?

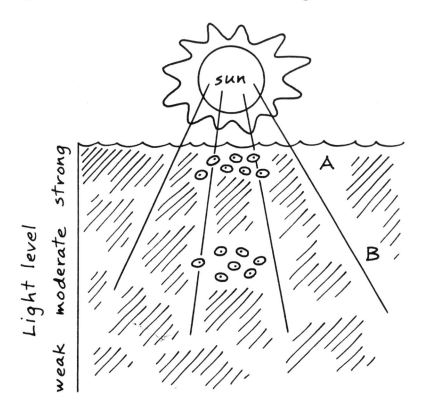

Answer

Think!

- Eyespots are useful in directing organisms toward moderate sunlight, but away from strong sunlight.

  The correct location for the organisms is location B.

Exercises

1. Study the diagram and determine which image, A or B, represents the monocular vision of most fish.

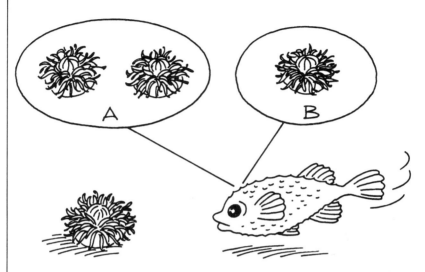

2. Study the eyes of the fish in the diagram and determine which type of eye would be best suited to fish in the most brightly lighted part of the ocean, near the surface.

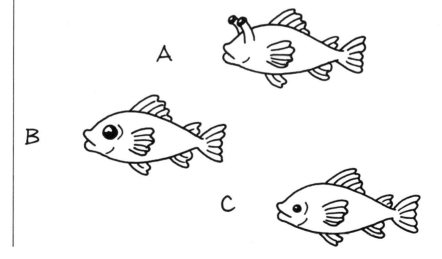

Activity: BACK AND FORTH

Purpose To show how fish eyes see objects at different distances.

Materials desk lamp
modeling clay
ruler
pencil
magnifying lens
masking tape
sheet of typing paper
small box, one side of which is about the size of the
typing paper

Procedure

NOTE: The distances given for the objects in this experiment will vary for different strengths of magnifying lenses.

1. Turn the desk lamp so that its light shines to one side.

2. Darken the room except for the light from the desk lamp.

3. Mold two stands from the clay, one walnut-size and one lemon-size.

4. Position the walnut-size stand about 12 inches (30 cm) in front of the lamp, and insert the pointed end of the pencil in the clay.

5. Position the lemon-size stand about 1 yard (1 m) in front of the lamp, and insert the magnifying lens in the clay so that the lens faces the lamp.

6. Tape the sheet of paper to one side of the box.

7. Position the box on the side of the lens opposite the lamp, with the paper facing the lamp.

8. Slowly move the box closer to and farther from the lens until a clear image of the pencil appears on the paper.

9. Move the pencil about 4 inches (10 cm) from the lamp.

10. Without moving the box, adjust the position of the lens so that a sharp image of the pencil again appears on the paper.

Results   When the pencil was moved farther from the box, the lens had to be moved closer to the box for a sharp image to appear on the paper.

Why?   Inside the eye of a fish is a small lens. Like the magnifying lens, the lens in a fish's eye is a **double-convex lens—** because it curves outward on both sides. This lens **refracts** (bends) light entering the eye and directs it to the area at the back of the eye, called the **retina.** The retina contains light-sensitive cells that change light energy into messages. Then these messages are sent along a **nerve** (special fiber that the body uses to send messages to and from the brain) called the optic nerve. The **optic nerve** carries messages from the eye to the brain, and the fish sees.

The eyes of a fish are similar to your eyes in many ways. However, there are certain differences, since a fish sees in water and you see in air. One difference is how the eyes adjust to seeing objects at different distances. In the human eye, muscles pull on the flexible lens, changing its thickness and thus its curved shape. The lens curves to a greater or lesser degree to focus on farther or nearer objects. Fish eyes work differently. The lens muscles in a fish's eye pull the lens back and forth to focus on distant and near objects. The movement of the magnifying lens in this experiment represents the movement of the lens in a fish's eye to focus the image of an object (the pencil) on the retina (the paper).

FISH EYE

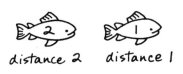

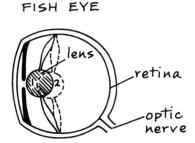

Solutions to Exercises

1. *Think!*

• With monocular vision, fish see separate images.

Image A represents the monocular vision of most fish.

2. *Think!*

* Tubular eyes (diagram A) and large eyes (diagram B) are found on fish in the deepest parts of the ocean, where there is limited light.

  Diagram C represents the type of eye best suited to fish near the brightly lighted ocean's surface.

25
Sensitive

Learning about the Sensory System of Fish

What You Need to Know

Like you, a fish receives information about the world around it through its brain, nerves, and spinal cord, which together form its **nervous system.** The **brain** is the control center for body actions and processes. The nerves are special fibers that the body uses to send messages to and from the brain, and the **spinal cord** is the large bundle of nerves running through the spine from the brain. In addition to the basic nervous system, a fish has special **sensory organs** (groups of special nerve cells) that detect changes in light, sound, water movement, and chemicals: the eye, labyrinth, lateral line, nose, and taste buds.

The eye of a fish is similar to yours in many ways, but there are differences that allow it to see in water, while you see in air. In your eyes, the **cornea** (the clear cover over the front of the eyeball) and lens both refract light rays as they enter your eyes. In fish eyes, only the lens refracts the light. Another difference is that your **pupil** (black dot-like opening in the center of the colored part of the eye) changes size, opening in dim light and closing in bright light. In most fish, the pupil stays the same size. It does not open in dim light and close in bright light as your pupil does. Your eyes have a **fovea** (the point on the back inside wall of the eye where images are focused). Most fish lack a fovea, which means their vision is not always clear. Fish do not cry, because they have no tear glands. The surrounding

217

water keeps their eyes moist. For more information about fish eyes, see chapter 24, "Lookers."

Fish do not have outer ears, but do have something similar to your inner ear. The fish's inner ear is called a **labyrinth.** Sound moving through the ocean water results in movement of the fluid in the labyrinth. Nerves report this movement to the fish's brain, and the fish hears the sound. The labyrinth, like your inner ear, also helps the fish balance. The movement of the fluid in the labyrinth tells the fish whether its head is up or down.

A special sensing system in fish that land-dwelling animals do not have is the **lateral line system.** It is made up of a series of sensory organs running along each side of the body and on the head of the fish. Each organ is connected to nerves. It is believed that this line of sensory organs detects pressure and sound that travels through the water. The lateral line is also used by the fish to determine its depth in the water, the presence of other moving marine creatures or objects, and its distance from them. As a fish moves through the water, waves move away from the fish's body. As the fish approaches an object, such as a rock or another fish, these waves are bounced back. The lateral line system detects the waves that hit the fish's body and enables the fish to avoid bumping into the object.

Fish smell with their noses. A fish nose, like your nose, has two nostrils. In a fish, water flows in one nostril and out the other.

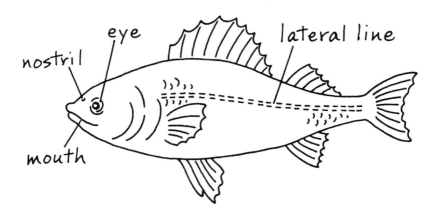

As the water enters, it stimulates nerve cells that tell the fish about odors. Many fish have such a keen sense of smell that they can detect very small amounts of chemicals in the water.

Fish taste with special nerve cells called **taste buds.** Your taste buds are located on your tongue. Most fish have taste buds scattered throughout their mouths and even outside their mouths on their lips. Some fish, such as the catfish, have taste buds on **barbels** (whiskerlike structures attached to a fish's mouth) as well as on their bodies.

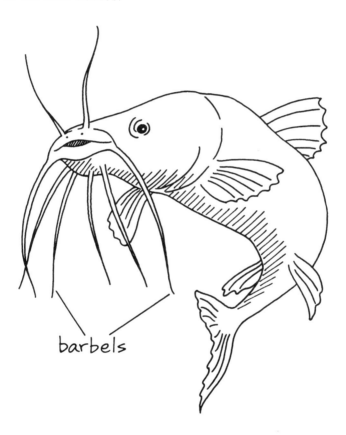

barbels

Let's Think It Through

Study the diagrams on the next page and select the one that correctly shows how the pupil of most fish eyes reacts to bright light.

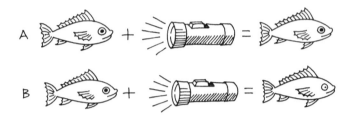

Answer

Think!

• The pupil in the eye of most fish does not change size.

Diagram A shows how the pupil of most fish eyes reacts to bright light.

Exercise

Study the diagrams and determine which sensory organs—eye, labyrinth, nose, taste buds, or lateral line system—are being used.

Activity: HEARING WITHOUT EARS?

Purpose To demonstrate how a fish hears without external ears.

Materials new, unsharpened pencil
dishwashing liquid
tap water
paper towel
helper

Procedure

1. Wash the pencil with dishwashing liquid and water, and dry it on the paper towel.

2. Place the unsharpened end of the pencil between your teeth.

3. Cover your ears with your hands.

4. Ask your helper to rub the eraser end of the pencil with his or her finger. Make note of any sound heard.

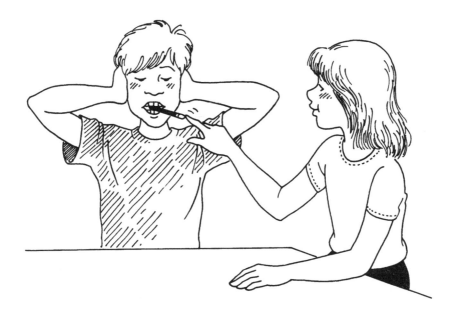

Results A loud scratching sound is heard.

Why? All sound is a form of wave motion produced when things **vibrate** (move back and forth repeatedly). Rubbing the pencil causes it to vibrate. As the molecules in the pencil vibrate, they bump into neighboring molecules and start them vibrating. These vibrations travel up the pencil to your teeth, through the bones in your head, and on to your inner ear. Fish do not have outer ears as you do, but do have something like your inner ear: the labyrinth. Vibrations from the water move through the bones of the fish's head to the labyrinth. Your inner ear and the labyrinth of a fish report sounds to the brain, where hearing takes place.

Solution to Exercise

Think!

- The chemical added to the water has an odor and a flavor. What organs in the fish detect odors and flavors?

  Fish A is using its nose to smell and its taste buds to taste the chemical being poured into the water.

Think!

- Waves from the body of the fish are bouncing off the coral and returning to the fish. What organ in the fish detects wave motion?

  Fish B is using its lateral line system to detect the waves bouncing off the coral.

Think!

- Light from the sun enters the water. What organ in the fish detects light?

  Fish C is using its eyes to see the worm on the fishhook.

Think!

- Humpback whales are known for the songs they sing. What organ in the fish detects sound?

  Fish D is using its labyrinth and its lateral line system to detect sound.

Glossary

abyss   The great depths of the ocean floor, generally with an average depth of 15,000 feet (4,500 m).

abyssal plains   The flat surface of the abyss.

air   A mixture of gases, made mostly of nitrogen and oxygen.

air pressure   The force air puts on an area.

algae   Plantlike organisms that contain chlorophyll and make their own food.

algal bloom   An excessive production of algae due to an increase in nutrients in the water.

altitude   The angle between a heavenly body and the horizon.

area   The size of a surface.

astrolabe   An instrument used to determine latitude.

atmosphere   The blanket of air that surrounds the earth.

baleen   Sheets of horny material that hang down from the upper jaw of the baleen whale and that are used instead of teeth to capture and eat fish.

ballast tank   A heavy tank used to stabilize and control the depth of a submersible.

barbels   Whiskerlike structures attached to a fish's mouth that are equipped with taste buds.

bathyscaphes   Diving machines that allow scientists to reach deep parts of the ocean.

bay   A part of a larger body of water that cuts into a shoreline, forming a curve.

beach   A shore with a smooth, sloping stretch of sand and pebbles.

benthos   All organisms that live on the ocean floor.

bioaccumulation   The process by which an animal gradually absorbs and stores a chemical in its body.

biodegradable   Able to break down into harmless substances by the action of living organisms, especially bacteria.

bioluminescence   The process by which living organisms produce light.

blowhole   The nostril on top of a whale's head.

blubber   Oil-filled threadlike tissue under a whale's skin that is used to keep the animal warm.

brain   The control center for body actions and processes.

breaching   The springing of a whale from the water.

breaker   A wave whose crest falls forward and crashes into the wave's trough.

calving   The process of iceberg formation.

cell   The smallest building block of all living things.

chemical oceanography   The study of ocean water and its chemical characteristics.

chlorophyll   A green pigment found in plants that is necessary for photosynthesis.

circumference   The distance around a circle or sphere.

cold layer   The bottom layer of seawater beneath the thermocline, in which the water is coldest and the temperature changes very little with depth.

compress   To squeeze together.

condensation   The process by which a gas changes into a liquid due to a removal of heat energy.

constellation   A specific arrangement of a group of stars.

consumers   Organisms that cannot produce their own food and must eat other organisms.

continental drift   The theory that all the earth's landmasses were once one single body of land that separated over many millions of years and drifted apart to form what we now know as the continents.

continental rise   The bottom area of a continental slope that gently rises above the abyss.

continental shelf   The area of the ocean floor starting at the shoreline and ending at the continental slope, where the water depth is approximately 667 feet (200 m).

continental slope   The steep slanted area between a continental shelf and the abyss.

continents   The seven major landmasses of the earth: North America, South America, Africa, Australia, Antarctica, Europe, and Asia.

contract   To draw closer together.

convection currents   The up-and-down movement of air or water due to differences in temperature.

corer   A hollow tube-type device that can be driven into the earth's crust to obtain a sample for scientific study.

Coriolis effect   The deflection of fluids as a result of the earth's rotation.

cornea   The clear cover over the front of the eyeball.

crest   The high point of a wave.

crust   The thin outer layer of the earth.

current meter   An instrument used to determine the speed of a current.

cyclone   A strong wind blowing in a circle; a hurricane in the Indian Ocean.

deep-sea zone   The area of the ocean floor beneath the waters in the open ocean.

deflect   To bend.

density   The "heaviness" of an object, based on its mass compared to its volume.

doldrums   The region of little surface wind near the equator.

double-convex lens   A lens that curves outward on both sides.

ebb tide   See **low tide**.

echo sounding   A method of determining distance by bouncing sounds off an object and listening for the echoes.

echo time   The time it takes sound waves to travel to an object, be reflected, and return to a sonar device.

endangered species   A species in immediate danger of becoming extinct.

environment   The surroundings of living things.

equator   The 0° latitude line midway between the North and South Poles.

erosion   The process by which materials of the earth's surface are slowly worn away, usually by wind or water.

evaporation   The process by which a liquid changes into a gas due to an addition of heat energy.

expand   To spread farther apart.

extinction   The dying out of a species.

eyespot   A light-sensitive area on an animal's body that is used to detect differences between light and dark.

family   A scientific grouping of organisms ranking below an order.

fathom   A measure of the depth of the ocean, equal to 6 feet (1.8 m).

fin   A usually flat body part on a fish that is used for movement and balance.

flood tide   See **high tide**.

fluid   A gas or a liquid.

fluke   The fin at the end of a whale's tail.

focus   To sharpen an image by use of a lens.

fog   A cloud, the base of which is on or near the ground.

food chain   A series of organisms linked together in the order in which they feed on each other.

food web   A number of interlinked food chains.

fovea   The point on the back inside wall of the eye where images are focused.

freezing point   The temperature at which a liquid changes into a solid.

freshwater   Water that is not salty.

friction   The force that slows the motion of two things that touch each other.

geological oceanography   The study of the ocean floor, beaches, and ocean fossils.

gills   Organs in a fish through which it gets oxygen from the water.

glacier   A large body of land ice that flows slowly downhill.

gravity   The force that pulls objects on or near a heavenly body, such as a planet, moon, or star, toward the center of the heavenly body.

guyot   A flat-topped seamount.

headland A projection of land that extends into deep water.

high An area of the atmosphere with higher air pressure than surrounding areas.

high tide Rising of the ocean's surface. See also **spring tide**.

horizon The imaginary line where the sky meets the earth.

hurricane A tropical cyclone with wind speeds of 74 miles per hour (118 kph) or greater.

iceberg A piece of the tongue of a glacier that has broken off into the sea.

insulator Any material that slows down the transfer of heat energy.

island A piece of land smaller than a continent and surrounded by water; a seamount that extends above the ocean's surface.

knot 1 nautical mile per hour.

krill A small shrimplike zooplankton.

labyrinth The inner ear of a fish.

land breeze A movement of cool air from the land to the ocean.

lateral line system A series of sensory organs running along each side of the body and on the head of the fish that is used to determine the fish's depth, the presence of other marine creatures and objects, and its distance from them.

latitude Imaginary lines that encircle the earth in an east-west direction and that are measured in degrees north and south of the equator.

lens The part of an organism's eye that focuses light rays by refracting light entering the eye and directing it to the retina; a piece of curved glass used to focus an image.

lithosphere The solid part of the earth.

low An area of the atmosphere with lower air pressure than surrounding areas.

low tide Falling of the ocean's surface. See also **neap tide**.

magma Liquid rock.

mammal Any warm-blooded animal with a backbone.

marine Having to do with the ocean.

marine biology The study of ocean life.

mass The amount of material in an object.

microscopic organisms Living beings that are too small to be seen with the naked eye.

Mid-Atlantic Ridge The section of the oceanic ridge that runs through the center of the Atlantic Ocean.

midnight zone The bottom layer of the ocean, which extends from the bottom of the twilight zone to the ocean floor and where light is produced only by bioluminescence.

molecule The smallest unit of a substance that retains all the properties of that substance.

monocular vision Separate images viewed by each eye.

monsoon A seasonal wind caused by temperature differences between land and ocean.

mountain range A string of connected mountains.

Nansen or **Nisken bottle** A tubelike device used to collect samples of water at specific depths.

nautical mile A mile as measured at sea, equal to 6,076 feet (1,823 m).

navigator Director of a ship.

neap tide   The lowest tide, produced when the sun and moon are at right angles to each other.

nekton   All organisms in the ocean that can swim.

neritic zone   The area of the ocean floor from the low-tide line to the edge of the continental shelf.

nerves   Special fibers that the body uses to send messages to and from the brain.

nervous system   The brain, nerves, and spinal cord.

Northern Hemisphere   The region of the earth north of the equator.

North Pole   An imaginary point on the earth situated at latitude 90°N and pointing toward Polaris; the area of the earth that is farthest north of the equator.

nostril   An opening in the head of an animal that is used for breathing and smelling.

nutrients   Substances needed for the life and growth of living organisms.

ocean   The entire body of salt water that covers about three-fourths of the earth's surface.

ocean current   A large stream of ocean water that moves continuously in the same direction.

oceanic ridge   A gigantic, continuous underwater mountain range.

oceanographer   A scientist who studies the ocean.

oceanography   The branch of science that studies all aspects of the oceans' physical features and inhabitants.

ooze deposits   Sediments consisting of dust particles from space, volcanic ash, dust blown seaward by winds, and sediments that drift down to the abyss from the upper levels of the ocean.

optic nerve The nerve that carries messages from the eye to the brain.

order A scientific grouping of organisms ranking above a family.

overharvesting Killing more of a species than can be replaced by reproduction.

Pangaea ("all land") The name given to the large, single landmass believed to have existed before the continents drifted apart.

Panthalassa ("all water") The name given to the large, single ocean believed to have existed before the continents drifted apart.

photosynthesis The food-making reaction in plants, using carbon dioxide, water, and sunlight.

physical oceanography The study of water movement in the ocean.

phytoplankton Plantlike plankton that are capable of producing food by photosynthesis and that are the most important producers in the ocean.

plankton Small, often microscopic organisms that drift with the current or tide at or near the ocean's surface.

plate A section of the earth's crust.

Polaris The star directly above the North Pole; also called the North Star.

polar regions The areas of the earth between 60° and 90°N and between 60° and 90°S.

pollutant A substance that destroys the purity of air, water, or land.

precipitation Liquid or solid particles of water that form in the atmosphere and then fall to the earth's surface.

predator   An animal that hunts and kills other animals for food.

pressure   A force applied over a certain area.

prevailing winds   The major wind patterns on the earth.

producers   Organisms, specifically plants, capable of producing food from nonliving matter.

pupil   The black dot-like opening in the center of the colored part of the eye.

raw sewage   Untreated liquid waste from drains, toilets, and sewers.

refract   To bend light.

retina   The light-sensitive area at the back of the eye where light energy is changed to nerve messages.

ridge   A mountain range. Under water, it is made up of trenches and seamounts.

rift valley   A central valley running the length of a ridge.

ROVs   *R*emotely *o*perated *v*ehicles.

runoff   The part of precipitation that washes from the land into bodies of water.

salinity   The measure of the amount of salt dissolved in a liquid, such as seawater.

saltern   A place where salt is produced by the evaporation of seawater.

scuba   *S*elf-*c*ontained *u*nderwater *b*reathing *a*pparatus.

sea   A large body of salt water that is smaller than an ocean and that may or may not be part of an ocean.

sea arch   A stone bridge-like structure that extends above the sea.

sea breeze   A movement of cool air from the ocean to the land.

sea cave   A hollowed-out place in a sea cliff.

sea cliff   A vertical rock wall that goes down sharply to the sea.

seamount   An underwater mountain.

sea stack   A column of rock standing in the sea near the shore.

seawater   Water from the ocean.

sediments   Materials that settle to the bottom of a liquid.

sensory organs   Groups of special nerve cells.

shelf break   The point where the continental shelf ends and the continental slope begins.

shore   The land at the shoreline.

shoreline   The area where the ocean and the land meet.

shore zone   The beach area, where the tides rise and fall.

solar process   The production of salt by the sun's evaporation of seawater.

solar salt   Salt produced by the solar process.

sonar   A method or device used to determine ocean depth or distances by calculating the time needed to send ultra-sound through the water and pick up its reflection.

sound   A form of energy that causes wave motion in materials it passes through.

sounding   An early method of measuring water depth.

sound wave   A disturbance in a material as sound travels through it.

Southern Hemisphere   The region of the earth south of the equator.

South Pole An imaginary point on the earth situated at latitude 90°S; the area of the earth that is farthest south of the equator.

species A group of plants or animals that are alike in certain ways.

sphere A ball-shaped object.

spinal cord The large bundle of nerves running through the spine from the brain.

spreading ridge A huge underwater mountain range created by the rising and cooling of magma in the ocean floor.

spring tide The highest tide, produced when the sun, moon, and earth are in line with each other.

spy-hopping The movement of a whale in a vertical position with its head out of the water.

strait A narrow body of water that joins two larger bodies of water.

subduction zone The area where crustal plates meet, one moving under the other.

submarine A submersible designed to operate under water for long periods of time.

submersibles Vessels capable of going under water.

sunlight zone The top layer of the ocean, with the most light and the most plant life, averaging 300 feet (90 m) in depth.

surface current An ocean current caused by wind.

surface layer The top layer of seawater, in which the water is warmest and the temperature changes only slightly with depth.

swim bladder An air-filled sac inside a fish's body that allows the fish to float.

taste buds Special nerve cells used for taste.

Tethys Sea The body of water separating the hypothetical landmasses of Laurasia and Gondwanaland.

thermocline The layer of water below the surface layer of the ocean, in which the temperature drops rapidly with depth.

tidal glacier A glacier, the tongue of which has reached the shoreline.

tides The regular rise and fall of the ocean's surface.

tongue The front, or lower, end of a glacier.

trench An underwater valley that is V-shaped, narrow, and deep.

tropical cyclone A cyclone that develops over the warm waters of the tropics.

tropical depression A spinning storm in the tropics with wind speeds of less than 39 miles per hour (62 kph).

tropical storm A spinning storm in the tropics with wind speeds of 39 to 73 miles per hour (62 to 117 kph).

tropics The area of the earth closest to the equator, extending from $23\frac{1}{2}°N$ to $23\frac{1}{2}°S$.

trough The low point of a wave.

tsunamis A series of freakishly long, high-speed waves caused by underwater disturbances, such as volcanoes, earthquakes, or landslides.

twilight zone The middle layer of the ocean, starting from the bottom of the sunlight zone and extending down to about 3,000 feet (900 m) below the surface, where there is little light, no plants, and few animals.

typhoon A hurricane in the northwest Pacific Ocean.

ultrasound High-frequency sounds that humans cannot hear.

vibrate To move back and forth repeatedly.

volume The amount of space inside an object.

warm-blooded Having a body temperature that does not change with the surroundings.

water cycle The cycle of evaporation, condensation, precipitation, and runoff that determines water movement between the atmosphere, oceans, and land.

water vapor Water in the gas state.

water wave A disturbance on the surface of water that repeats itself.

wave height The vertical distance between the crest and trough of a wave.

wavelength The horizontal distance between similar points on two successive waves.

weather The condition of the atmosphere in a specific place at a particular time.

weight The measure of the downward force of an object toward the center of the earth due to gravity.

wind A generally horizontal movement of air.

zooplankton The animal form of plankton.

More Books about Oceanography

Billett, David. *The Usborne Book of Ocean Facts.* London: Usborne Publishing Ltd., 1990.

Fun facts about the ocean. Easy to read, with cute, colorful diagrams.

Center for Marine Conservation. *The Ocean Book.* New York: John Wiley & Sons, 1989.

Very easy reading, with simple diagrams and fun activities about the ocean and the plants and animals that live in it.

Groves, Don. *The Oceans: A Book of Questions and Answers.* New York: John Wiley & Sons, 1989.

A book written for people with a general interest in oceans. Slightly technical in a few places, but requires no special qualifications of the reader. A very thorough and informative book about the world's oceans. Extremely helpful in studying basic oceanography.

Laver, Barbara. *Sea Life.* Huntington Beach, CA: Creative Teaching Press, 1987.

Very easy to read, with large, simple diagrams. Contains facts and activities about sea life.

McGinley, Avalyn. *Oceanography.* St. Louis, MO: Milliken, 1984.

Informative, with simple diagrams and easy-to-read activities.

Morris, Rick. *Mysteries and Marvels of Ocean Life.* London: Usborne Publishing Ltd., 1983.

Short, easy-to-read, fun book about life in the ocean.

Nature Scope. *Diving into the Oceans.* Washington, DC: National Wildlife Federation, 1992.

Good general information book, with simple, interesting black-and-white diagrams about the ocean and ocean life.

Pernetta, John. *Rand McNally Atlas of the Oceans.* London: Reed International, 1994.

A very informative atlas of the oceans, with colorful diagrams and photographs. In addition to the thorough information, the book is just fun to look at.

Wells, Susan. *The Illustrated World of Oceans.* New York: Simon & Schuster, 1991.

A very informative book, with many action-packed, colorful diagrams.

Williams, Brian. *The Sea.* New York: Kingfisher Books, 1992.

A simple, easy-to-read book about the sea and its contents. Beautiful color diagrams of sea life and sea activities, including how man may live under the sea in the future.

Index

Abyss:
    abyssal plains, 50, 225
    definition of, 50, 225
    illustration of, 49
    model of, 53–55
    ooze deposits, 55, 232
Antarctic Ocean, 14
Arctic Ocean, 13, 14, 15
Astrolabe:
    definition of, 30, 225
    model of, 27–30
Atlantic Ocean:
    early navigation of, 24
    hurricanes, 149
    map of, 15
    size of, 13, 14
    volume of, 18–21
Atmosphere:
    air in, 65, 225
    air pressure, 65, 225
    definition of, 65, 225

Bathyscaphes, 33, 225
Bay:
    Bay of Biscay, 16, 17
    definition of, 16, 225
Bioaccumulation, 138, 226
Bioluminescence, 166, 226
Beaches:
    color of, 88
    definition, 87, 226
    old, 87
    size of, 87
    young, 87

Challenger, H.M.S., 31, 34, 38, 39
Challenger Deep, 34

Constellation, 24, 227
Continental drift, 6, 227
Continental rise:
    definition of, 50, 227
    illustration of, 49
Continental shelf:
    boundaries, 49
    definition of, 49, 227
    illustration of, 49
Continental slope:
    definition of, 50, 227
    illustration, 49
Continents:
    definition, 6, 227
    distribution of, 5–11
    map of, 15
Corer, 41, 227
Coriolis effect:
    definition of, 73, 227
    model of, 70–74
Cousteau, Jacques, 32
Current meter, 42, 227
Currents:
    convention, 65, 107–110, 227
    ocean, 42, 159, 232
    surface currents, 65–75, 236
Cyclone, 149, 238

Doldrums, 149–150, 228
Drebell, Cornelius, 37

Earth:
    continental drift, 6, 9–10, 227
    continents of, 6, 227
    crust, 6, 227
    equator, 24, 228
    horizon, 24, 230

Earth (*cont'd.*)
   latitude, 24, 25, 26–30, 230
   lithosphere, 95, 231
   magma, 6–7, 231
   Northern Hemisphere, 13, 232
   North Pole, 24, 232
   oceans of, 13–22
   plates of, 6, 233
   polar regions, 65, 233
   Southern Hemisphere, 13, 235
   South Pole, 6, 24, 236
   subduction zone, 7, 236
   tides, 95–102
Endangered species, 137, 228

Fathom, 39, 229
Fish:
   barbels, 219, 225
   fins, 190–191, 229
   flounder, 184–186, 208
   gills, 198, 229
   illustration of, 191
   labyrinth, 218, 230
   lateral line system, 218, 230
   sensory system, 217–224
   swim bladder, 191, 193–195, 236
   vision of, 208–214, 217–218
Food chain:
   consumers of, 173–174, 178–179, 229
   definition of, 173, 229
   predators, 145, 234
   producers of, 173, 178–179, 233
Food web, 173, 229
Fulton, Robert, 37

Gagnan, Emile, 32
Glaciers:
   calving of, 157, 226
   definition of, 157, 229
   formation of, 157
   tidal, 157, 237
   tongue of, 157–158, 237
Gondwanaland, 6

Hurricanes:
   definition of, 149, 230
   formation of, 152–154
   names of, 149

Icebergs:
   color of, 158–159
   definition of, 157, 230
   location of, 159
   position in water, 158, 160, 161, 162–164
   size of, 158
   sources of, 159
Indian Ocean:
   map of, 15
   size, 13, 14
   volume of, 18–21

Knot, 46, 230

Land breeze:
   definition of, 148, 230
   illustration of, 148
Latitude:
   definition of, 24, 230
   determining, 24–30
Laurasia, 6, 8, 11

Marine life:
   benthos, 166, 226
   bioluminescence, 166, 226
   eyespots of, 207, 228
   flatfish, 184–186, 208
   food chain, 173–180, 229
   mammals, 198, 231
   movement of, 189–196
   nekton, 165, 232
   ocean environment, 165–171
   ocean floor, 181–187
   overharvesting of, 139, 233
   phytoplankton, 165, 176, 233
   plankton, 165, 233
   plants, 166, 170–171, 173
   sensory system of fish, 217–224
   vision of, 207–215
   warm-blooded, 198, 238
   whales, 197–205
   zooplankton, 165, 173, 174, 238
Maury, Matthew, 31, 32
Mid-Atlantic Ridge, 51, 231
Monsoon, 148, 231

Nansen bottle, 41, 231
Nautical mile, 46, 231
Northern Hemisphere:
    definition of, 13, 232
    map of, 14

Ocean:
    abyss, 50, 225
    Antarctic Ocean, 14
    Atlantic Ocean, *see* Atlantic Ocean
    beach, 87–88, 226
    Challenger Deep, 34
    continental rise, 49, 50, 227
    continental shelf, 49, 227
    continental slope, 49, 50, 227
    currents of, 42, 159, 232
    definition of, 5, 232
    depth of, 57–63
    distribution of, 5–11
    diving suits, 32, 33
    divisions of, 13–22
    early studies of, 23–30
    floor features, 49–56
    food chain, 173–180
    icebergs, 157–164, 230
    Indian Ocean, *see* Indian Ocean
    marine life, 165–224
    modern studies of, 31–38
    Pacific Ocean, *see* Pacific Ocean
    Panthalassa, 5, 233
    pollution of, 129–136
    salinity of, 121–128
    scuba gear, 32, 234
    shoreline, 87–94, 235
    surface currents of, 65–75, 236
    Tethys Sea, 6, 237
    thermocline, 103–104, 237
    tides, 95–101, 237
    vessels of, 32–37
    water pressure, 113–120
    water temperature of, 103–111
    waves, 77–85
    weather affected by, 147–155
    zones of, 166–167, 181–182
Ocean floor:
    depth of, 57–63
    features of, 49–56

    illustration of, 49
    marine life, 181–187
    model of, 53–56
    ooze deposits, 55, 182, 232
Oceanic ridge:
    definition of, 50, 232
    illustration of, 51
    measurements of, 51
    Mid-Atlantic Ridge, 51, 231
Oceanography:
    chemical, 32, 226
    definition of, 32, 232
    geological, 32, 229
    marine biology, 32, 231
    physical, 32, 233
    tools of, 39–48
Overharvesting, 139, 233

Pacific Ocean:
    area of, 14
    Challenger Deep, 34
    map of, 15
    size of, 13, 14
    typhoons, 149, 237
Pangaea:
    animals on, 7–8
    definition of, 5, 233
    distribution of, 5–11
    Gondwanaland, 6
    Laurasia, 6
    location of, 6
    map of, 5
Panthalassa:
    definition of, 5, 233
    distribution of, 5–11
    map of, 5
Photosynthesis:
    chlorophyll, 171, 226
    definition of, 165, 233
    example of, 170–171
Plates:
    definition of, 6, 233
    motion of, 7
    subduction zone, 7, 236
Polaris:
    definition of, 24, 233
    use in navigation, 24–30

Pollution:
  algal bloom, 135, 225
  bioaccumulation, 138, 226
  biodegradable, 129, 226
  effect on marine animals, 137–145
  ocean, 129–145
  raw sewage, 130, 234
  runoff, 135, 234

Salinity:
  definition of, 121, 234
  ocean, 121–128
Scuba:
  Cousteau, Jacques, 32
  definition of, 32, 234
Sea:
  definition of, 16, 234
  map of, 18
Sea breeze:
  definition of, 148, 235
  illustration of, 148
Seamount:
  definition of, 50, 235
  guyot, 50, 229
  island, 51, 230
Shelf break:
  definition of, 50, 235
  illustration, 49
Shoreline:
  beaches, 87–88, 226
  definition of, 6, 235
  effect of waves on, 87–101
  headlands, 88, 92–94
  sea arch, 89, 234
  sea cave, 89, 235
  sea cliff, 89, 235
  sea stack, 89, 235
Solar process:
  definition of, 127, 235
  example of, 126–127
  saltern, 127, 234
  solar salt, 127, 235
Sonar:
  definition of, 39, 235
  echo time, 40, 57, 228

  measuring ocean floor with,
    57–63
  ultrasound, 39–40, 237
Sound:
  definition of, 40, 235
  ultrasound, 39–40, 237
  waves, 40, 235
Sounding, 39, 235
South Pole, 6, 24, 236
Southern Hemisphere:
  definition of, 13, 235
  map of, 14
Strait:
  definition of, 16, 236
  Strait of Gibraltar, 16, 17
Submarine:
  ballast tanks, 37, 225
  definition of, 37, 236
  model of, 35–37
Submersibles:
  bathyscaphes, 33, 225
  definition of, 32, 236
  examples of, 35
  ROVs, 32, 33, 234
  submarine, 35–37, 236
Surface currents:
  definition of, 67, 236
  direction of, 67–75
  production of, 65–75

Tethys Sea, 6, 237
Thermocline:
  definition of, 103, 237
  illustration of, 104
Thomson, Charles Wyville, 31
Tides, 95–101, 230, 231, 237
  cause of, 95–101
  definition of, 95, 237
  high, 95, 230
  low, 95, 231
  model of, 98–101
  neap, 97, 232
  spring, 97, 232
Trenches, 7, 237
Typhoon, 149, 237

Water cycle:
   definition of, 147, 238
   illustration of, 147
Waves:
   breaker, 78, 226
   crest of, 78, 227
   effect on shoreline, 87–94
   height, 79, 238
   movement of water, 78, 83–85
   sound, 40, 235
   trough of, 78, 237
   tsunamis, 79, 237
   water, 77–85, 238
   wavelength, 78, 79, 238
Weather:
   definition of, 147, 238
   fog, 147, 229
   hurricanes, 149, 230
   monsoon, 148, 231
   oceans' effect on, 147–155
   precipitation, 123, 233
   tropical cyclone, 149, 237
   tropical depression, 154, 237
   tropical storm, 154, 237
   typhoon, 149, 237
   water cycle, 147, 238

Wegener, Alfred, 6
Whales:
   baleens, 197, 225
   blowhole, 199, 226
   blubber, 198, 203–204, 226
   breaching, 190, 226
   echo sounding, 199, 228
   families of, 197
   flukes, 198, 229
   senses of, 199–200
   spy-hopping, 190, 236
   vision of, 199, 209
Wind:
   cyclone, 149, 228
   definition of, 65, 238
   direction of, 65–66
   doldrums, 149–150, 228
   land breeze, 148, 230
   monsoon, 148, 231
   movement of, 65–67
   prevailing, 65, 67, 234
   sea breeze, 148, 235

Zooplankton:
   definition, 165, 238
   krill, 165, 230

**Get these fun and exciting books by Janice VanCleave
at your local bookstore or fill out the order form below and mail to:
John Wiley & Sons, Inc., 605 Third Ave., NY, NY 10158**

Janice VanCleave's Science For Every Kid Series
___Astronomy   53573-7 $10.95 US / 15.95 CAN
___Biology   50381-9   11.95 US / 16.95 CAN
___Chemistry   62085-8   10.95 US / 15.95 CAN
___Dinosaurs   30812-9   10.95 US / 15.95 CAN
___Earth Science   53010-7   11.95 US / 16.95 CAN
___Ecology   10086-2   10.95 US / 15.95 CAN
___Geography   59842-9   10.95 US / 15.95 CAN
___Geometry   31141-3   10.95 US / 15.95 CAN
___Human Body   02408-2   10.95 US / 15.95 CAN
___Math   54265-2   10.95 US / 15.95 CAN
___Oceans   12453-2   11.95 US / 15.95 CAN
___Physics   52505-7   10.95 US / 15.95 CAN

Janice VanCleave's Spectacular Science Projects
___Animals   55052-3 $9.95 US / 12.95 CAN
___Earthquakes   57107-5   9.95 US / 12.95 CAN
___Electricity   31010-7   9.95 US / 12.95 CAN
___Gravity   55050-7   10.95 US / 14.95 CAN
___Machines   57108-3   9.95 US / 12.95 CAN
___Magnets   57106-7   9.95 US / 12.95 CAN
___Microscopes &
Magnifying Lenses   58956-X   10.95 US / 14.95 CAN
___Molecules   55054-X   10.95 US / 14.95 CAN
___Rocks   10269-5   9.95 US / 12.95 CAN
and Minerals
___Volcanoes   30811-0   9.95 US / 12.95 CAN
___Weather   03231-X   9.95 US / 12.95 CAN

Two VanCleave Science Bonanzas
___200 Gooey, Slippery, Slimy, Weird &
Fun Experiments   57921-1 $12.95 US / 16.95 CAN
___201 Awesome, Magical, Bizarre &
Incredible Experiments   31011-5 $12.95 US / 16.95 CAN

Janice VanCleave's A+ Projects
___A+ Projects in Biology   58628-5 $12.95 US / 17.95 CAN
___A+ Projects in Chemistry   58630-7   12.95 US / 17.95 CAN

[   ] Check / Money order enclosed   (Wiley pays postage & handling)
[   ] Charge my: _____Visa   _____Mastercard   _____AMEX
Card #_____   Exp. Date _____/____
Name: _____
Address: _____
City / State / Zip: _____
Signature: _____
(Order not valid unless signed)